another
hysterical
female

by kristin giese

Printed in the United States of America
First Printing, 2022
ISBN 978-1-7339927-5-6
all moxie ink

www.anotherhystericalfemale.com

This book is a work of creative nonfiction, and the stories told herein are told to the best of the author's recollection. Memories are not linear, nor are they perfect. To that end, some of the material will stretch for stories sake. For continuity purposes, some events have been compressed while others have been omitted altogether and dialogue has been recreated to further the story's arc. Details, where faded from memory, have been conjured for the page. Some names and identifying details have been changed or left off the page altogether to protect privacy. The theories, takeaway, and lessons in the book are meant to help, empower, and embolden the reader toward expansion. The author is not a therapist nor a medical professional in any way and, thus, the advice herein is not a replacement for mental health or medical treatment. The publisher and the author assume no responsibility for inaccuracies, omissions, or any inconsistencies herein and hereby disclaim any liability to any party for any loss, damage, or disruption caused by errors or omissions, whether such errors or omissions result from negligence, accident, or any other cause.

For Merna.

I still see you everywhere.

PROLOGUE

"We'll pull the ten baby teeth that haven't fallen out, attach wires to the bicuspids so we can yank 'em into place, and then put braces on the teeth remaining. Easy peasy," the oral surgeon explained with a broad smile.

My best guess is, most malpractice suits begin with testimony that includes, "and then the doctor said, 'easy-peasy, lemon-squeezy' before leaving a scalpel in my lower intestines."

Thanks to the surgeon's described cake walk of a procedure, I had spent the past three weeks trapped in a dental hellscape with a dry socket cherry on top, subsisting solely on soup, Knox Blox, and *Three's Company* reruns.

Today, I was returning to school and my sixth-grade class.

"I can't walk with these," I complained, hobbling into my elementary school on the crutches my mom had rented earlier that morning at the drugstore downtown.

"I thought her mouth was the problem," a classmate whispered to our teacher as they passed us by in the hall.

He wasn't wrong. My mouth *had* been the problem, but last night I fell running up the stairs and "deeply stubbed my toe," as medically diagnosed by my mother.

"These don't work," I whined.

"That's because they're not tall enough for you. Here," my mom said, pulling the right crutch out from under my arm. Unprepared, I stepped forward and put all my weight on my sore foot. I blanched and slumped to the floor just outside my classroom.

For a fleeting moment, I saw my mother's commitment to her stubbed toe theory waiver, but she recovered quickly by shoving a Jell-O packet into my hand and dragging me to my desk.

Mrs. Michaelson, my 6th grade teacher, eyed us suspiciously from her perch at the back of the room. I smiled weakly, eating cherry gelatin as my mom hauled a step stool from the chalkboard to elevate my leg.

"Stubbed toe," my mom mouthed to Mrs. Michaelson, as explanation of the scene we were making.

At three o'clock, I hobbled out to the curb and fell into the front seat of our minivan.

"Toe better?" my mom asked as she drove to the orthodontist.

"A broken foot doesn't heal in a day," I chided.

She rolled her eyes. "You're so dramatic," she said, a statement for which she had quite a few receipts.
I've always had a flair for theatrics. In preschool my teacher pinned a note to my backpack that read, "Please talk to Kristin. She's declared herself a crocodile and has bitten two classmates and one teacher."

I like to believe I'm a pit bull in business, today, because in my formative years I tasted the blood of weaklings.

"I see you have hoof and mouth disease," the orthodontist joked as I crawled into the dental chair. I didn't laugh, in part because the only thing worse than dad jokes are dentist jokes, but also because the new rubber bands in my mouth hurt too much to smile.

"I think I broke it," I said through gritted teeth.

"You think?" he questioned.

"We're not sure." I shrugged.

Without warning, he reached down and tugged off the sock that was delicately covering my toes. I yelped in pain. He gasped. The top of my foot had turned jet black.

"Cheryl!" he shouted to reception, "get Mrs. Giese back here. She needs to take her daughter to the hospital."

"Why didn't you tell me it was black?" my mom hissed as she folded me into the front seat of the van, embarrassment still flushing her face.

"I told you it was *broken*. You didn't believe me," I challenged as she shoved my crutches in the back.

She glowered at me.

"I didn't know it was black, okay? That's new information to us both," I admitted.

At the Urgent Care, the doctor took one look at my black foot and hauled me into the Xray room.

Ten minutes later he returned with an *actual* medical diagnosis, unlike my mother's.

"It's broken. The 4th and 5th Metatarsal, to be exact. We can't set it. It's been too long. We're worried about blood flow. You need to go straight the hospital emergency room. They may need to re-break it."

I turned the last sentence over in my mind, horror building inside me. I couldn't tell you, then, what I thought he meant when he said it, but ten years later my vision played out in *Misery* when Kathy Bates hobbled James Caan with a sledgehammer.

I leveled my eyes at my mother, raised my hand, pointed at her, and said, "You're a *horrible* mother."

Even the doctor looked hurt by my verbal assault.

"I knooooow," my mom wailed in response, hysterical. Two nurses immediately fled to her side to console her.

"She always breaks her toes, you know?" my mother said, lifting her eyes to one of them.

They agreed. The nurses understood. One of them gave *me* a dirty look.

"And we've gone three times to the ER in the past. They always say you can't do anything for a broken toe. Right?"

The nurses nodded in solidarity. "Right," one shushed.

"Plus, she's so dramatic, like, all the time." My mom hiccupped from crying.

"They always are," a nurse hushed as she rubbed my mom's back.

Then, my mom looked at me, her quivering lip growing into a full cry as a shame-spiral of mom-guilt engulfed her.

A third nurse rushed in with orange soda to comfort her.

Of course, my mom wasn't wrong about any of it. I'm a Gemini daughter with a Leo moon rising. I have been in my feelings since the birth canal. Tack on sarcasm since preschool, a wild ability for storytelling since kindergarten, and a size six shoe in the third grade, and you get someone who doesn't need a stubbed toe to turn any situation into a sideshow.

My mom was doing the best she could, which was pretty darn good. She's an amazing mom, but I have been hysterical my whole life, in all senses of the word. I am funny. I am emotional. And as someone who plays big even when others are demanding I be small, I have been labeled hysterical plenty of times by those who don't know what else to do with a strong woman other than cut her down.

This book is about the hysterical parts within me, within ALL of us.

I've come to believe that trauma, despite all the earnest talk that surrounds it, might actually *be* a laughing matter in that if we — at some point — don't find a way to laugh again, we have lost more to our trauma than it has earned from us.

For years, I thought I was *just* a closer. It's a part of my job to get the deal. But, as I've unfolded as a producer, writer, storyteller, I've come to realize that, while I can and do close, I *thrive* that much more as a fixer.

It's a role I've had since the start of my career. In fact, *fixer* is at the top of the food chain of my task list. I have always been the first line of defense to solve whatever problem was in front of us.

So, that's what this book is. Mostly funny stories from my life to fix us.

I have cherry-picked stories from my childhood, my life in entertainment as a talent manager, publicist, and producer, and the things I've learned running my own company to shed light on how what hurts us can also point us toward what will radically heal us.

We've shown that we're strong enough to vulnerably cry about it, and don't get me wrong, crying is good, necessary, needed… Heck, I cried twice last week just for shits and giggles.

But from one hysterical human to another, I want to now see if we're brave enough to laugh about it.

ONE

Headset and Weight Belt

I took my vibrator to Best Buy.

Because climate change. Duh.

I don't have any data that tells me my masturbation habits are linked to the plight of the polar bears, but I don't think now is the time to be cavalier. The ice caps are melting, People.

So, I did what I believe Leonardo DiCaprio would want me to do...would want us all to do, really...I took my Magic Wand vibrator to Best Buy to be recycled.

For those of you that don't know, the Magic Wand is the Mercedes of vibrators. *Wirecutter*, the independent review section of *The New York Times*, picked it for their top slot. I figured, I trusted them with my Christmas tree and toaster oven selections, why not my vagina, right?

The publication said their reviewers put 110 hours into testing the category. Not sure how that went over with HR, but I needed only two *minutes* to know they were right about *this* and the Cuisinart Convection Oven. You're welcome.

Here's what I've learned. My philosophy on vibrators is pretty similar to cars. Keep 'em clean, lubed, and charged; and every few years it's good to upgrade. Obviously, this goes without saying, while it's okay to lease your Volvo, NOT your vulva. Vibrators are an owned-only category. Please and thank you.

So, I took Riggs to be recycled. Yes, I named him. I've also named my oven, curling iron, and washing machine. Although, admittedly, I've never been to third base with any of them...yet.

I'm not a monster, so I wrapped Riggs in an ULTA bag because they're peach and opaque. Honestly, if I weren't choosing to have my ashes sprinkled along the Amalfi Coast as my bon voyage to this earth, I'd pick a peach coffin, too. Peach lacquer feels like the exact, big shoulder pad energy I want for my entrée to the afterlife.

I planned my route carefully. Coffee, post office, FedEx pick up, and then a Riggs drop off on my way home.

Now, I'm not saying that the customer service is lacking at Best Buy, but also, have you been?

I once tried to buy a washing machine there. I explained to a sales associate what I was looking for — front load, cycle options, dependable.

He pondered, and said, "I've got just the model for you. This way."

I followed him through the store, weaving through aisles of DVDs and surround sound speakers.

"This has everything on your list." He smacked his hand down on the white metal of the machine and smiled proudly, his Blackberry holstered at his hip.

I looked down at the Whirlpool appliance before me, its powder-coating shining brightly under a ceiling of fluorescent lights.

"Isn't that a dishwasher?" I asked.

He looked at it blankly. "What's the difference?"

"Only everything," I said.

He bristled, "This isn't my department," and walked away.

And, that right there is why when I needed to buy a dryer last year, I bought "Doug" at Lowe's.

But, *today,* as I approached the entrance to the store, I wasn't worried. I had no reason to think anyone would even notice my arrival.

The doors swished open. Cold air blasted out creating the customary retail weather pattern of 95-degree heat on the sidewalk and artic, air-conditioned air in the store. I stepped in and strode toward the large, cardboard recycling bins sitting dutifully at the far end of the vestibule, mausoleums to dead batteries, burned-out game controllers, and, as of today, *probably*, their first vibrator.

I focused on my task, as women saving the environment are wont to do. Perhaps that's why I didn't notice the blue-shirted zealots of this super store ascending upon me, that is until they had surrounded me.

I made eye contact with one of them. *Connor*, his name tag read.

"Can I, like, help you?" he asked, a *Bill & Ted* inflection to his tone.

He was flanked by two colleagues, neither had nametags. I'll call them Headset and Weight Belt, based on their attire.

I looked down at the peach bag in my hand. They did too. *Shit.*

"Are you, like, recycling that?" Connor asked.

"No," I said assessing the distance from them to the door and the freedom just beyond. I was like Jason Bourne casing the exits, except his penis is attached. Mine was in my right hand.

"Are you sure? I'm, like, happy to take it off your hands." Connor reached out and made contact with the bag.

Here's the thing, I don't know if a tree falling in the woods makes a sound if no one is there to hear it, but I do know that if you take a vibrator to Best Buy in a bag and hand it to someone, *even* if they don't know they're holding said vibrator, it's a thousand percent a sex crime. It's not been covered on *NCIS*, but it's the best guess I have.

Connor gently pulled the bag from my hands.

I can't say for sure, but when I let go, I think I yelped. Their eyes collectively widened at me. I coughed, attempting to cover the awkwardness.

Spoiler, it didn't work.

"So, what do we got here?" Connor asked, testing the heft of the bag.

For a second, I thought he might open it and peer inside. I was ready to fly at him like a spider monkey if he tried it.

"Just so I can put it in the right bin," he justified.

I looked at him blankly.

Connor, Headset, and Weight Belt stared back at me.

"An alarm clock?" I answered as more of a question.

Connor squeezed the bag, "Seems thin for an alarm clock," he observed.

My heart literally stopped.

"I don't have a lot of space on my nightstand, Connor," I said with what must have felt like an odd amount of defensiveness.

"Mine's the same," Headset offered.

I framed my face as someone who wasn't suddenly terrified that he meant the contents of the bag and *not* his bedside furniture.

"Good enough," Connor said, "You sure you wanna give it up?" he asked holding it over the bin.

I nodded, willing this torture to end.

I watched as he angled the bag several different directions, turning it this way and that to make it fit down in the hole.

Trust me, the irony was not lost on me, either.

"Should we say a few words?" he asked.

I looked stricken.

"Maybe, just a moment of silence," he concluded with a smile.

My knees were buckling.

They each faced the green carboard tomb and bowed their heads. I did, too, but that was because I was praying not to get arrested on a major felony charge before lunch.

Then something *truly* unexpected happened — which is saying a lot considering the scene. Weight Belt began to mouth-trumpet the melody to "Taps."

And that, my friends, was the last time I went to Best Buy. Mostly because I'm afraid of jail, but also because it's hard to top a military burial for your vibrator.

Why am I telling you this?

Because, up until telling this story, I have never, in my life, spoken a word about masturbation to anyone. In fact, I didn't even own a vibrator until I was 28.

When I finally worked up the courage to buy one, I didn't just throw the packaging away. I tore it up with a pair of scissors so my neighbors wouldn't accidentally see the box in the trash and deduce, "I bet *it* belongs to that perpetually single pervert in 3A."

As I've gotten older, though, I've come to realize that all the stuff we don't talk about, be it sex or our sadness, at some point goes from secrets to shame.

Well, guess what? We're done with shame.

But *saying* we're done and *being* done are two totally different things.

To truly change a feeling, I believe we need to shift the behavior that abets it, because feelings and behaviors are intrinsically intertwined.

Simply put, emotions go in, behaviors come out, and our life follows suit.

Think of it like a vending machine. If we're the customer, we only get two options. Put coins in and choose from what's inside to come out. Patterned behavior creating predictable emotional outcomes.

But what happens if we decide we want to shift that paradigm? What if we aren't *just* the customers? What if we become the owners? *Ownership* is the difference between the options we *have*, and the options we *create*. *Ownership* means we're in charge of choosing how we're going to behave and how we're going to feel. Those are two pretty big variables to place on the scales of fate. I'm not saying that we can control everything that happens to us. I am, however, saying we can decide how we respond to it.

When we own our behaviors, we create better emotional outcomes. When we expand our emotional understanding of ourselves, we heal our behaviors.

Each of us has a vending machine. Our buttons don't read Bugles and Sunkist Grape. They are our narratives. My most common narrative is unworthiness. I have put so much damn money into *that* machine. The same quarter going in, hoping for Orange Crush, but buying the self-belief that I'm not enough, not what most men are looking for, too fat, too much, too focused on my career, and on, and on, and on....

We *all* run our lives like a poorly stocked vending machine from time to time. Unhappy about our choices, resentful about getting the wrong outcome, and wanting our money back. But that's end-of-the-distribution-chain thinking. We bought the company, remember? That means we get to decide who runs the trucks, what stock they carry, and how much it costs to buy our inventory.

That means we are in charge. So, if your mother-in-law is selling emotional KitKats off the back of the van, she loses her route. She's stealing. We're vending machine tycoons. We don't let people who are robbing us blind, emotionally or otherwise, run amuck in our lives or businesses.

Put that on a sign and hang it in the breakroom.

Maybe we can't fire her entirely — that whole you married her son or daughter situation — but we can give her a new job, one with way less say in how we run this empire.

We're founders now. We have to step it up. We have to change the behavior that keeps us hurt. In my case that means talking about it.

I'll go first. Listen up, Shame....

I took my vibrator to an undisclosed Best Buy and laid it to rest. I'm sure it went against at least a dozen health codes, a few state laws, maybe even one or two federal, and probably every HR policy Best Buy has, but it taught me something about life.

First, and very importantly, don't take your vibrator to Best Buy. While there is no shame in having one, having sex, not having sex, loving who you love, and being proud of your sexuality, I can't imagine that Best Buy's recycling program is ready for today's modern feminists to drop off their mini vibes at their front door. I'm guessing we should stick with our broken printers for now.

Second, my mom may have come from the generation that didn't talk about any of this. Sex, shame, body issues, depression...it was all said in whispers. But she *did* always say, "Nothing gets done around this house unless I do it myself." And if that isn't the Yelp review on self-healing summed up in one line, then I don't know what is.

So, I'm going to start by writing about all of it.

I always tell my clients, "Don't tell me who you are, make me *feel* who you are." This book is that in action. My best bet is that when I make you feel *me*, you'll feel more *yourself*, too.

I've just got to believe that if we can put a man on the moon, we can certainly put our pain, trauma, and fears into orbit and let them go. Unashamed. No apologies.

Unless your names are Connor, Headset, and Weight Belt. To you three, specifically, I am deeply sorry and will forever hope that you never looked inside that ULTA bag.

TWO

Wax On, Wax Off

"I don't really get *waxed* but thank you," I said graciously, smiling at my new HR director.

I could tell by the way she was looking at me, this wasn't the right answer.

"Well, *we* all go. So, if you change your mind, you'll get 30% off," she shrugged. The long ash hanging of her cigarette broke free and fell into the massive printer on her desk.

The early 2000's were a different time.

I walked back to my office and sat down. *This* was what I had dreamt of for so long, a job in the city, a corner office, and clients all my own.

"You got some good ones," a voice said from the door. I looked up and followed her gaze to the pile of office supplies I had just raided from the supply room. She picked up the stapler and clicked off two staples from the metal hammer. Two bent frames fell to my desk. I mourned for them.

"I thought so," I smiled, and gingerly took the cherry Swingline from her hands.

"I'm so excited to work together. I'm just down the hall." She gave a wave and was gone, her Bvlgari perfume hanging in the air as the only proof that she had been there.

I protectively moved the stapler to the opposite side of my desk. Sequestered, I now admired my new status symbol, its red body declaring its dominance, and mine somehow, over all the grey staplers on the 19th floor. Office supply hierarchy is real.

I've never snorted a rail of cocaine before, but I *have* been handed a stack of pushpins and my first box of business cards. So, I think I get the idea. I admired my name now hanging on my corkboard.

Getting *anything* waxed was the furthest thing from my mind. I'm from Ohio, the birthplace of the mullet....and I don't mean on your head. Up until an hour ago, I had never even considered the topic, but now I had a growing voice in my head that said, *"Do whatever you have to, to fit in."*

I peered at my eyebrows in my mirror. The brows on the faces of the other women in the office were as groomed and full as an Afghan Hound. Mine were wispy and unimpressive. They screamed, "Beagle!"

I looked at the card in my employee welcome folder and called to make an appointment.

I had never before had a job that made me feel important, but when I told the woman on the phone where I was calling from, she moved my three-week out appointment to the next day. Power felt good.

I wrote the appointment and each of her instructions into my brand-new Franklin Covey planner.

"I'm getting my eyebrows waxed tomorrow," I told my mom on my ride home.

"Why? Don't you have tweezers?"

Every family has its firsts. First to college. First to move away. I would be the first to get my eyebrows done. Truthfully, it felt obscene. I barely had enough cash to pay my rent, but I wanted to belong. That meant looking the part even if I didn't *feel* the part.

I was small town, hand-me-downs, garage sales, and public pools, while my new officemates were big city, country clubs, Chanel bags, and Louboutin heels. This appointment felt like I was taking the first step in becoming more like them, and I *wanted* to be more like them.

The next morning, I arrived to work and stashed my lunch in the office fridge. In an endless barrage of salads and

Diet Cokes, I was a salami on white bread with mayo and cheese. I had a lot of catching up to do. Portion controlled plastic containers and romaine went to the top of my mental shopping list.

"Heard you're seeing Marta today," my boss said as she passed me in the hall. "Don't worry, she's got magic hands. Doesn't even hurt."

Until she said it, I hadn't even registered that it *would* hurt.

At 11:30 a.m. I swung the door open to the spa. The smell of essential oils washed over me as the receptionist handed me my first chilled cucumber water. One sip and I knew the days for my drugstore St. Ives Apricot Scrub were numbered.

A few minutes passed when a stoic woman appeared in the doorway. "Christina?"

I looked up. "I'm Kristin," I said.

She just turned and walked down the hall.

As she walked, she said, "Says eyebrows on chart, but all girls from office do full kitten. You do too, yes?" She phrased it like a question, but somehow it wasn't.

"Sure." If all the girls in the office were doing it, then so was I.

She swung open a door and pointed to the bench. "Just robe. Then lay on table."

Fear engulfed me as I changed. When the door swung back open, I raised my head to stare at her. I was entirely unsure of how this whole waxing shebang even began.

"Put leg on shoulder," she commanded.

That is what, I believe, they call a plot twist. I can honestly say that whatever I imagined was going to be first step, it wasn't *that*.

I wanted to protest, but terror is a tricky business. You either run or crawl into the trunk of your own accord. In I went.

Not surprisingly, it's hard to make small talk when your leg is draped over a stranger's shoulder.

The left side went off without a hitch — silent, painful, but uneventful. Then she swapped to the other side. Awkwardly, I put my leg onto her shoulder. She swirled the tongue depressor through the hot wax and applied it to my skin. Next, she covered the wax with fabric strips before pressing them into place and eventually ripping them off.

Marta had a lot to do. My role was easy. Clench.

Then, she went in again, lower this time.

That's when it happened. She tsked. I don't really ever want to hear anyone tsk when they're looking at a nude body part of mine, but it felt especially confronting since it was my labia.

"What?" I asked, my head popping up off the table.

"Nothing," she said. But, then she tsked again.

I looked at her, pleadingly. "Tell me," I begged.

"Is just, the right side of your vagina is lazy. You know this, yes?"

She stared at me.

"Yes," I said, breathlessly.

Spoiler alert, I didn't know. I *still* don't know. It's been twenty years and I remain completely in the dark on this diagnosis.

My entire body went numb.

"*Lazy!*" I said to myself, turning the word over and over in my mind as Marta continued her now-rueful, full kitten. "*What does that mean?*"

By the time she moved on to my eyebrows, I was in a full, emotional death spiral. It took all I had in me not to cry.

I returned to the office a shell of my former self, but with *really* good brows. So, there was that.

I closed my office door and raced to open Google. Everyone else was searching, plane tickets, vacation weather, and the tip off time for the big game. I came in hot with, "What's a lazy vagina?" and "What do you do if you have one?"

Let me be very clear. Do not google this. It won't be helpful. Trust me. WebMD has very little to say on the topic. Pornhub, however, has a lot to tell you. None of it is relevant, not even the guy named Todd who declares that he's just the guy who knows how to whip your lazy Lady J into place. Todd, I assure you, is not qualified.

I turned the phrase over in my mind a thousand *more* times, oddly in Marta's accent.

With the internet being zero help, I thought about where I could turn next. *Who can I ask?* I thought. A *friend?* I cringed at the idea.

"Hey, girl! Your pics from Hawaii looked amazing! Question, is either side of your vagina lazy?"

That was going to be a clear no. Not surprisingly, there just aren't very many openings in a conversation where you can inquire about your best friend's labia.

So, I decided I was in an anatomical spelling bee. I would break it down.

I know what being lazy is, I thought. That didn't seem helpful. I delved deeper. *What are <u>other</u> things that are lazy?*

The first item that popped into my mind was a Lazy Susan. If you don't know, a Lazy Susan is a plate you put into the middle of your table that spins. Often it has different dishes and a center component for dips.

For the ladies in the room, I want to be clear about something. My vagina does not spin. And, while I know we've just met, I need to know right now if yours does. Because if so, I am *really* far behind on what this advanced piece of machinery can actually do.

Then, I thought, *What about a lazy eye? Are they connected? Is my right eye just going to roll in at some point?*

I felt panic gripping me at my desk.

When I got home, I stood in front of my mirror and gave myself the Coach Taylor pep talk of my life. If "Clear Eyes. Full Hearts. Can't Lose," can work for football players, I had to believe it could work for my lazy vagina, right?

I said aloud, "You are a badass. She's an idiot. What does she know anyway? You're driven and focused…at least 95 percent of you is," I trailed off and then began to cry.

I had only spent 20 minutes with Marta, but those 20 minutes would haunt me for twenty years. That's the rub about shame. It sticks to you until *you* peel it off.

I have no idea what Marta meant. For all I know, she could have been building up to sell me a vajazzling, rejuvenation session. All of it could have been a sales tactic.

But, as women, our bodies are objectified, compared, shamed, and picked apart each day in a million ways. My mind diagnosed this immediately as *just* another way in which my body was less than.

This wasn't Marta's fault of course...not entirely. My body being *bad*, being a source of shame had started decades before. Marta was just my brain's way of continuing and confirming that narrative, as our brains are wont to do.

My mom always said, "If you go looking for trouble, you'll find it." I like to think that if our brains had a license plate, that would be the state slogan, right next to a picture of Michael B. Jordan, because who needs a state bird when we can have *him,* right?

For me, the shame of my body began when I was nine. It was when I found out I was fat. Up until that point I had no idea. It's partly because I *wasn't* actually fat, but my grandmother thought I was and *that* was all that mattered.

"Was ist das denn?" she asked in German. She was my dad's mother, and my whole life we called her Oma, the German word for grandmother. "You eat so much," she judged, as we sat at breakfast, me eating the apple fritter, ironically, she had given to me. "You're getting so fat," she chastised, grabbing a chunk of my waist and squeezing.

Her criticisms grew into comparisons. "See these girls," she'd said pointing at my friends, "they're not fat. Don't you want to be like them?"

Then the put-downs picked up real inertia, and their G-force pulled in *other* elements, "You aren't pretty enough to be fat. No one will ever marry you." "Why are you so tall? Don't you hate that?"

She was a real thrill ride, my oma.

Point is, the shame I was made to feel about my body had cut bone deep, long before Marta got her hands on it.

Now that I'm an adult, I've come to understand something about what hurts us.

Pain is a pattern; one we repeat again and again and *again* until we heal it. That is the salve that finally breaks the pattern. That is what scabs the pain.

When I met Marta, I hadn't healed it yet.

Maybe as a middle-aged woman, I still haven't healed it, but I'm getting closer.

I know this. I have repeated the relationship with my oma with at least two other people. Cruel putdowns. Slights. Emotional hostage taking. They read like the greatest hits of a low self-esteem national tour. It's a bop we all know.

I, of course, didn't realize *that* when I was in those relationships, but looking back I see it now. I was repeating the pattern of my relationship with her, with others, because I hadn't learned the lesson from how she hurt me and how it taught me to hurt myself.

Then a shift happened. I realized this: If you are in a relationship with someone whose bigness is predicated upon your being small, you are in the wrong room, Boo. You need to exit stage left immediately.

First, we are all meant to play big. Swing for the fences. Summit the mountain. Get the win. Anyone who makes you doubt that does not deserve your energy, heart, or help, even if it's your own subconscious. Maybe *especially* if it's your own subconscious. Show him or her the door.

The truth about trauma's muscle memory is this: We don't *even* need the person who hurt us to continue doing the hurting. At some point, we take it up all on our own accord.

I had severed the relationship with my oma. In fact, she's now dead. But even though she wasn't in my life regularly, I still lit the torch of that shame all on my own.

Trauma is good like that. It's like a gift. Someone gives it to you, but, here's the clincher, at some point you get to decide if you keep unwrapping it. Maybe you want to be like me and sign yourself up on a lifetime registry for that which hurt you and fricking unwrap it each day. Like I said, trauma can be fun like that.

Several years ago, though, I decided I wouldn't be doing that any longer.

But once you say, *'Enough!'* you have to get yourself off the bridal registry of your own pain. Up first, we have to name what has hurt us. The seed of it. The core. We're all very good at treating the branch, but I'm talking about identifying the trunk. By that I mean, when you tell me you are angry or jealous or shameful. I will tell you that is a branch. Fear is the trunk. We need to go there, to the core of what it was, name it, and own it, in order to heal it.

When my oma said I wasn't pretty or good enough to get a man, I decided then, *'Well, if I can't have that fairy tale, if I can't be Princess Diana, I'll just have the career and the handbags, instead. <u>Those</u> I can build for myself.'*

So, that's what I did. I shut off the personal side of me and became professional Kristin, even as a kid. Other girls envisioned their wedding day, their one true love. I was thinking about being a fashion buyer at Bergdorf's and the jewelry I'd find at a Paris flea market on a business trip.

I flung myself after my career goals, all outfitted in my best black dress, drapey silk kimono jacket, and vintage Fendi with a statement necklace for good measure. And I built the career I wanted, but, big surprise, not the personal life I told myself I didn't need.

That's because I was afraid *she* was right. I was terrified *she knew* I wasn't worthy of being loved. So, I shut that part of myself down before I had the chance to confirm it. That's my trunk, ladies…and maybe, even, a few gentlemen readers.

Sometimes we crawl so far out on the limb of our lives and get so high in our branches that we lose sight of our trunk. We go on treating our *symptoms* but not our *source*. Worse yet, we become ashamed about the whole damn tree.

Hugging our tree trunk is the way we heal all that. It's the way we claim our shadows so that we can grow towards the sun once again.

At least, that's what I think.

Once I realized, *everything* is just a decision away, I took up a line of thinking anchored by this belief: Our behavior is an outcome, but our emotion is the origin. And, just like every superhero, the origin story is where it's at as far as healing is concerned.

Here's a big, blinking, neon sign that I've passed again and again in my origin story.

We get what we fear.

It's because fear, like everything else, has a vibration. I think we, as humans, actually have two frequencies, our head and our heart vibration. We vibrate at both, but the Universe listens to just one.

We have mastered the head voice. *It's all good. I can handle this. I got this. He's worth the wait. I can stop...*and so on.

That's what we're listening to and acting upon.

But the Universe is Netflixing and chilling, little and big spooning, and sambaing with our solar plexus vibe. That is where we hold our fear. Our head distracts us from it. It has us building treehouses, connecting oaks, chopping branches...but the Universe is hugging our trunk, listening to all that vibrational hot gossip of all that we fear and pulling it *right* towards us. And, as it comes our way, we keep turning our branches into firewood and burning our own house down, blaming it on the leaves, on life, on loved ones, but the trunk is *ours*.

I think it's time we all come down out of the trees, place our hands over our hearts, and ask ourselves what we really fear. Deep down we know, and when we take *ownership* for what we hear and meet it with kindness, grace, abundance, and love, we finally stand a chance to heal it.

Otherwise, it's just another day and another *someone* weed-whacking the bush of our pain. In Marta's case, that bush was both literal *and* figurative.

THREE

Let's Put a Pin in It

Text chains hit differently as we age. It starts innocently in our late 20s with, *"From here on out, I'm ONLY day drinking."*

In our 30s it escalates a smidge to, *"Need a physical therapy rec. Pulled my groin sleeping. Don't ask."*

By the time we hit our 40s, though, things really pick up steam. *"Do you think Advil will help with my hemorrhoid?"*

Aging is fun.

Not that it's all bad. What we lose in hormones, we make up for in wisdom.

For one, we stop caring as much about what other people think about us. It's like we've spent our lives carrying the weight of someone else's opinions around in our respective purses or gym bags. In our 40s we realize *this isn't my jock strap* and leave it in the lost and found.

I feel especially lucky to have had a mom who told me early on not to listen to the haters, or as she and every mom in the 80s put it, "Those kids are just jealous of you, Honey."

But, with the advent of social media, that gets harder and harder to remember. Our days are filled with the opinions of others, hurled at us publicly in the comments or, worse, anonymously in our DMs. It's exhausting.

I thank my lucky stars that social media wasn't around when I was in high school.

In the ninth grade, I swallowed a corsage pin. You read that right. I, Kristin Giese, swallowed a corsage pin. Three inches long. Pearl on one end.

I was a choreographer for the chorus line in our school's talent show. It was opening night of a two-night run. The girls had given the other instructors and me corsages for our respective jacket lapels.

Later that night, I decided it would be nice to wear the corsage again for night two. My mom and I were in our kitchen talking about all the backstage gossip as I carefully wrapped it back in its plastic as preparation to keep it overnight in our fridge. I held the corsage pin in my mouth like a seamstress might her straight pins, talking out the left side of my mouth as the other held the pin in place. It was autumn. I had a dry cough and red eyes due to my annual battle with allergies due to autumn's falling leaves. Suddenly, I had a coughing fit. I inhaled dramatically, and that's when it happened. I inhaled the pin.

I felt it instantly. It lodged into my windpipe. My mom's eyes widened in terror. Mine did, too. I was choking, clutching my throat. Like a Navy Seal on the front line, my mom swung me around and did the Heimlich. The pin shot up and stabbed me in the roof of my mouth. I screamed and spun back toward her.

"Iiiiinnnn," I screamed, my tongue holding the thin sliver of metal in place against the roof of my mouth.

"GRAB IT!" my mom shouted hysterically.

With my thumb and index finger, I reached in and grasped the metal, its daggered end stabbing into me. Tears streamed down my face. I could taste blood. I heard my mom shouting, "No no no no no no no...," as I involuntarily swallowed. The pin slipped from between my fingers and was gone.

I breathed heavily, my fingers resting on my lower lip, staring ahead in a daze.

My mom grabbed my shoulders and shook me, "Where's the pin?"

I didn't respond. I was in shock.

"We're going to the hospital," she said as she grabbed my hand and pulled me to the door.

My dad fell to the ground, combing the rug for the pin. "It's got to be here. Who swallows a pin?" he said in disbelief as she dragged me out.

I sat hunched forward in the front seat of the car as my mom swerved through our small town.

"Why are you sitting like that?"

"I don't know," I said. She accepted this and drove faster.

She slammed on the brakes at the entrance to the ER. I flung forward in my seatbelt and gurgled a whimper as I flew into the dash.

"You can't park here," a nurse shouted through the glass window at me, his cigarette smoke cloudy in the night air.

"My daughter swallowed a corsage pin!" my mom shouted.

His eyes bulged. He flung the door open, unbuckled my seatbelt, and hauled me out.

By the time my mom parked and was inside, I was on a gurney, in route to radiology for X-rays.

I returned 20 minutes later in a gown, robe, and booties, the pin still inside me.

"So, you're our human pin cushion," a nurse cooed as she settled me in. "Don't feel bad. People ingest all kinds of things around here. Just had a woman swallow a toothbrush last week. She fell running to the door to get the pizza guy. Went halfway down. She swallowed it the rest of the way."

I started to hyperventilate.

The curtain flew back, and a doctor strode in. He walked directly to the wall, slid the X-ray into a panel, and turned on the light board. There, plain as day, was the pin, pearl down, at the top of my intestines.

"We're glad to see it in that position. Not as stabby that way," he offered as a medical assessment. "We're gonna let you pass it."

My mom actually cackled.

"Is that funny?" the doctor asked.

"Oh, you're serious?" she questioned. He nodded blankly. "You can't let her pass it. It could stab her intestines or something or puncture her stomach or worse."

I couldn't imagine worse. I paled and started to feel faint.

The doctor stared at her. I could tell that he was annoyed by my mother telling him what to do, but also considering her words.

"I'll be right back," he said.

As soon as he left, my mom hissed, "Is he *crazy*? You can't pass a corsage pin."

I lay back on the gurney. I was going to pass out or bleed internally from a ruptured stomach. Or both, according to my mother.

The curtain swung back open. "Okay, we're prepping to get it out with a scope."

"What does that mean?" I asked sitting up. A nurse pushed me back down on the gurney, preparing an IV.

"It means I'm going to take a scope and put it down your throat and fish the pin out." He looked at my mom. She nodded her consent. They were a team now, it seemed.

With her approval, the doctor waved the nurses into action. One rushed forward with a syringe which she proceeded to inject into my IV.

"Are we sure about this?" I asked nervously of my mother, already feeling the effects of whatever the nurse had just administered.

All the activity in the room slowed and then stopped as everyone waited for my mother to answer. *What is she, like, the director of the ER now,* I thought.

My mom stepped forward, put her hand on my head, leaned in, and said lovingly, "You don't want to poop out a corsage pin sideways. Trust me."

Not exactly the last words you want to hear from your beloved mother as you're whisked down to surgery.

Hours and lots of nitrous gas later, with my stomach emptied of all its contents and my throat on fire from singing "Respect" 85 times with an endoscope down my esophagus, the doctor emerged and told my parents he had retrieved the pin. He even asked them if they wanted it. Monsters that they are, they said no. My best guess is that it now hangs on the doctor's wall in a shadowbox, right next to a Hall of Fame baseball that he *also* didn't earn.

I woke up feeling like I had done 80,000 sit ups. The doctor informed me that he'd played cat and mouse with my corsage pin for four and half hours. I had sung Aretha Franklin the entire time, despite having a scope down my throat.

"I actually had to tell you, *if I don't get the pin on the next pass, I'm cutting you open.* That perked you up. You asked what you could do. I told you *stop singing, stop moving, stop breathing if you can help it,* think only of me getting that *pin.* I guess you did because two seconds later, I had it," he said, proudly.

As a sidebar, I know this story isn't about my manifesting skills, but I'd like to point out that even under heavy nitrous gas conditions, they're Jedi strong.

All this to say, I'm intensely happy that the internet wasn't around for the pin-cident to have been hashtagged. Can you imagine the Instagram hazing I would have endured had the school known? They would have skewered me with my own, ingested corsage pin.

Fact is, it is intensely hard to practice *not* caring what other people think about you when you're trending.

The social stigma of swallowing a corsage pin prior to Instagram was being emotionally *maimed*, which I will take a thousand percent over being *meme'ed*, which is what would have happened today.

It's somewhat ridiculous when you think about it. We're all trying not to care what others have to say about us while at the same time posting a picture of our breakfast and praying it gets likes and shares. The irony of that is staggering.

But in your 40s, something happens. You realize you can take it all in stride or not at all. Not everyone and everything we pass on our journey needs to become a passenger on our life's road trip.

Things *can* be left right where we found them. Not only that, we don't have to keep returning to them over and over again. It doesn't serve us well. It's like our lives are these long road trips, and our 40s are when we realize that if we keep driving back 100 miles, every 30o miles, we're never going to get to where we want to go.

And that's what we're doing, emotionally speaking, when we return to these moments in our past again and again. They keep us tethered within a 50mile radius of our pain.

At some point we slip behind the wheel and realize, if we really, truly want to make progress, we have to pull over, right now, and either fix the piece of us that is broken, forgive it, or leave it on the side of the road like a flat tire that is slowing us down. Otherwise, we're just circling *not* continuing.

Life requires continuing.

The truth is, what has hurt us holds us back most when *we* insist upon that part of us remaining hurt.

Freedom is found not in healing our pain but in liberating ourselves from the idea that we *are* our pain. We are so much more than what has hurt us.

I know some of you might argue that. You might say there are realities out of our control. It's true, but so is this. Life is a series of choices. Some are made *for* us, some are made *against* us, but neither of those has the same authority as the ones made *by* us.

Accountability is heavy. That's what makes it so easy to drop, and we do. We put it down. We pass it off. We leave it at baggage claim going round and round on the luggage carousel. *"Not my bag"'* we say. *"That was done to me."*

But what was done *to* me is always trumped by *and so this is what I did about it*.

In the case of social media, I set some ground rules. I decided Instagram, Tik Tok, Facebook, and all the others would be a tool I use to connect to a community I am building. It would not be a tool that can be used against me to take me apart. And there will be people who will try to take us apart, because so often our success, joy, happiness, and abundance becomes an affront to those who haven't fought hard for their own.

When that happens, I will kindly pull over, open the door, and leave them on the side of the road to fix their own pain, because when people come *for* you it is almost always to put their pain *onto* you. But what they project upon us does not reflect us. It is a mirror for them. It is a mirror for their pain. It is a mirror for their pattern. Attacking you shows that they left their accountability at baggage claim, while you and I were busy grabbing our Louis rollers and heading right out the door with ours.

FOUR

The Neighborhood Welcome Wagon

"I'm gonna go introduce myself to the new neighbors."

My mom looked up, eyeing me suspiciously through her owl-sized glasses, "Alone?" she asked.

"Yup."

"So what, you're the neighborhood 8yr old welcome committee?"

"Someone has to do it."

She pursed her lips. "And that someone is you?"

I shrugged.

She flipped the page of her Penney's catalogue as I willed her to say yes.

"Say hello and come right back," she said without even looking up.

I was off like a shot, screen door slamming, my clogs clomping on the cement, as I ran down our street toward their house.

When people ask me today how I got my start in producing reality television, I tell them it was here — I've been low-key spying on my neighbors since I was eight.

I reached their sidewalk, the third to last house on the block. I didn't know anything about them, really, other than the fact that *he* went to work each day and *she* didn't. Laundry appeared on their line, flowerpots emerged on their front porch, but *she* was nowhere to be found.

Weeks of pedaling my hand-me-down bike around our block left me obsessed with this *young* couple and who they were, especially her.

"He's handsome. What do you think *she* looks like?" I asked my mom days earlier as we sat watching "Another World," our summertime afternoon ritual.

"Who?" she asked, absent-mindedly folding laundry, her eyes not leaving Felicia on the TV screen.

"The wife of the new couple down the street."

"There's a new couple down the street?"

I rolled my eyes and left the room.

"Take your laundry!" she shouted after me.

I flopped down on my bed and grabbed my notebook. I wrote FACTS at the top of a clean page of white paper before proceeding to list all of the clues I had collected thus far.

Young
He works
She doesn't

I looked at my list. Clearly, a Nancy Drew I was not.

"What do you think she does? I bet she's cool," I dished as my dad and I cleared supper plates. "And him," I said, clearly impressed. "They're young, you know? How old do you think they are?"

"Who?" my dad asked.

"The new neighbors." *Does no one listen to me around here?*

"The ones with the baby?" he questioned.

"*Baby?*" I spun to face him.

"Yeah, I think they have a kid."

I dropped my sponge and raced upstairs, leaving my dad at the kitchen sink. I pulled my notebook out. 'Baby,' I wrote on the list of clues. My investigation had just escalated.

Five days later I stood huffing and puffing on their front porch, my finger hovering centimeters from their buzzer. I felt nervous, half wanting to solve the case, half wanting to keep the mystery alive.

I pushed the button. When the door creaked open, I launched into my rehearsed speech.

"I'm Kristin, your neighbor. I live down the street. That way." I pointed. "I don't know if anyone welcomed you, but I wanted to say hi."

The woman stared at me, blinking, then craned her neck to see if an adult was with me.

"Anyway, we don't see you much, so I thought I better just stop by. Say hi. See how you're doing. See how you're liking the neighborhood," I fished.

Nancy Drew would be proud, I thought.

"Well, the neighborhood seems nice," my mystery neighbor began cautiously, no doubt still suspicious of the strange kid clad in a terrycloth romper and Dr. Scholl's on her front porch. "But honestly, I don't get out much with Riley."

I nodded as the woman spoke, willing myself not to jump through her screen door and snoop through her coffee table.

"Who's Riley?" I asked, trying to play it cool.

The woman stepped aside so I could see inside the tiny living room behind her. *There* a little girl lay propped up on a wedge bolster on the floor in the middle of the room, toys and a blanket spread out around her. She had casts on both her legs.

"Is that your baby?" I asked, staring past her to her daughter. I could see the little girl's face illuminated by cartoons on the TV screen.

"She's not exactly a baby. She's almost two."

I looked up at Riley's mom. She was beaming so brightly at her daughter that light rays were almost shooting out of her eyes.

"Is she hurt?" I asked, noting the bolster and two casts, one on each of her legs.

"Riley has brittle bones," the woman said matter-of-factly.

My kid brain didn't know what that meant, but I knew it wasn't good.

"Can I say hi?"

Riley's mom paused. "You can, but you can't touch her. Okay?"

The heat of the room surprised me when I stepped inside. It was late spring. The windows should have been wide open, but instead it was a furnace in their family room.

Riley's mom must have seen my reaction because she offered this answer without being asked, "We keep it warm. The less we fuss with clothes the better. Right Ry?"

Riley's mom looked down at her daughter. I did, too.

Riley stared back up at both of us. Her eyes were huge, emerald green saucers, and her hair was thick and deep as cherry wood.

"Hi!" Riley said, shimmying her way to the edge of her

bolster, a doll in her outstretched hand. "Hug," she demanded, both her arms reaching out for me.

I could feel Riley's mom tense, worried that I might lean in. I instantly felt like I wanted to cry, but I didn't want her mom to see that. So instead, I took Riley's doll and embraced it in an exaggerated hug.

Peals of laughter escaped from Riley. She clapped her hands. The lump in my throat expanded to match her joy.

"I have to go," I said suddenly, feeling like the tears in my eyers were going to spill over. I handed Riley's doll back to her and stood. I rushed to the screen door only to surprise myself by turning back around. "Can I visit again tomorrow?" I asked.

Riley's mom stared at me like she were a pour of soda bubbling over in too small a cup. "I think we'd like that," she said.

I returned the next day and for many after that, visiting Riley off and on that entire summer.

"Read," she would demand, shoving a book in my hands. I loved the way she always held me tightly with her long fingers, their swollen joints like the bulbed tips of a tree frog's toes. And, while Riley always wanted to hold onto me physically, I could feel her mother holding me in another way.

"I think Riley's mom is happy when I visit. She always stares at me and smiles, like, real big," I told my mom while we cooked dinner.

"I'm sure, but I think it might be a bit more than that. I think she's happy Riley has a friend. Every kid needs friends, maybe especially Riley," my mom said, shaping a meatloaf in a casserole pan.

I'm sad to admit that I don't know what happened to Riley and her mom.

They moved away. I grew up.

But I think about that summer, and then I think about all of us. I think about how we can each be so fragile and so fierce at the same time. We forget that we can be more than one thing. In fact, we can be opposite things at the same time. A masterpiece *and* a work in progress. Lost *and* found.

I think about times in my life, when I was completely terrified of what I was about to do while being simultaneously certain that it was the right move to make. Like the end of a friendship where you are gutted that it is over, but glad to be done with the person who is hurting you.

Riley is a reminder that being fragile does not mean being weak. Thanks to her, I came to believe that the most vulnerable parts of us house the deepest wells of our strength.

As adults, we don't put our buckets down those wells. We become leery of them. But we wouldn't be if we knew that, bucket after bucket, that's where we'd find the endless source of our grit, determination, truth, and fight.

Riley had many broken bones in the short time I knew her. I've only ever officially broken one, my foot. The same foot I mentioned before, which I broke in the sixth grade.

Ultimately, I had to wear a cast for weeks. It went from the base of my toes all the way up to my knee. When the cast came off, and I saw my calf and foot, I was horrified. Both were gangly and thin, and oddly pale grey in color.

"Stand on it," the doctor instructed.

I was terrified. "It's gonna break," I said as shakily as I stood, clutching the papered bench next to me.

"You'd think so by looking at it, but broken bones are always stronger than regular bones. The cast did its job. You have to trust it now. You have to know it's stronger *because* it healed. In fact, if you overprotect it, that's how you'll get hurt elsewhere. So, you have to run full out."

Funny fact about that doctor's advice. He was talking about my shattered foot, but as an adult, I have applied it to my shattered heart.

We do so much to over-protect what we are afraid is broken within us that other parts and pieces of us get damaged in the process. But what if we stopped believing our brokenness needs to be protected and instead started believing it needs to be trusted?

After all, it has steeled us in so many ways.

I think the reason we don't is because there is a hamster wheel to trauma, and it goes like this: We protect what we don't trust, and what we don't trust, we can't heal.

I didn't trust that I was worthy of being loved, so I protected myself from what, exactly? LOVE? As crazy as that sounds, yes.

Why would I do that?

I think the answer, indirectly, lies in something my foot doctor said in 1986.

When we protect our pain, we steal from our possibility.

Now, I'm no Nancy Drew, but doesn't it feel like I just solved my first mystery? Maybe?

FIVE

Birds of a Feather

"I think that man wants your attention."

I was down on bended knee looking at a blanket filled with handmade, Native American jewelry pieces in downtown Santa Fe. Still kneeling, I twisted around and looked back over my shoulder. A man rushed toward me, waving.

I stood up.

"There you are," he said, a broad smile on his face, as he broke free from the crowd. "I think this is the feather you were looking for, right?"

I looked down to his hand to see that he held a wide-band, sterling silver feather bracelet. And, just like that, my world cracked in half.

Three weeks earlier, I had awakened bleary-eyed and dazed in my Chicago loft, groping in the dark for my phone. My nightstand alarm clock blinked 7:48 a.m.

I punched my mom's number into my mobile.

"It's Saturday. What?" she answered gruffly, still half asleep.

My dad and I are the morning people in our family.

"I had a dream we went to Santa Fe for a feather."

"When are we going?" she asked without skipping a beat.

"We?"

"If I'm in the dream, I'm on the plane, especially since you woke me at 6 a.m. to tell me."

"It's almost eight." I said, dryly.

"I want an aisle seat," she said with a yawn. "But right now, I'm going back to sleep." The line clicked off.

I padded to the kitchen, my cat Jersey hopping off the bed in pursuit of me and kibble. As I made coffee, I searched flights.

I had started my company, all moxie, six years earlier. In that time, I had planned events in Milan for fashion week, worked with dozens of major broadcast shows, carried out national media hits, written hundreds of press answers, called the paparazzi on behalf of celeb-requested captures, and completed a zillion other accomplishments that, honestly, I had no idea how to do until I was doing them.

What I had *not* done was taken a day off.

I was in pursuit of my dreams, and they were in sight. *You don't take your foot off the gas when you're climbing the hill,* I told myself as I missed holiday trips home. *This'll all be worth it. You're working extra hard now so that later you can enjoy what you've built,* I would remind myself as I crawled into bed, bone-tired after cross country trips or late-night deadlines. *You won't have to put up with these people forever. Eventually, you'll pass them by on the road to the top,* I would tell myself after dealing with yet another, demanding executive partner.

I didn't have office hours. There was no point. It was my company. That meant I worked 24/7. There wasn't a weekend when my phone *didn't* ring. As if on cue, it buzzed in my hand, startling me.

"What the fuck are you even thinking?" I heard as soon as I punched accept.

I knew enough by who it was on the other end of the line and their *tone* that this was not a question I was meant to answer. Instead, I waited for them to continue. "I'm reading your email, and I'm disgusted."

I heard the phone click to speaker. Apparently, there was now an audience to my reprimand.

"I think it's safe to say that we're all disgusted. Right? I mean, I'm not the only one who saw this email come in and thought what the actual FUCK is Kristin thinking, am I?"

I heard a muffled acknowledgment of agreement from the peanut gallery in the room.

A new voice crackled over the line, "Honestly, I'm shocked that you didn't just say no...that you didn't know *enough*, by now, to just say no. I mean, why would you even think about doing this? I don't get it. If anyone else here knew about this...well, talk about destroying a partnership. My God. Is that what you're trying to do?"

Another question that was not meant to be answered. Take note, narcissists don't seek answers, they set traps. Always.

This call was solely to let me know that they'd already caught me in a snare. Defending, explaining, excusing myself wouldn't free me. It would just be me chewing off the *wrong* leg.

"I'm happy to say no," I began, calmly. "I didn't share it because I hoped you'd say yes. I sent it over because it's my job to do so. I'm not here to make assumptions and I'm not making *any* decisions. I'm just making certain I have your perspective. That's my goal. Obviously, conversations come up. I felt like you would all want to be in the loop on each of those. Was I wrong in *that* thinking?"

The silence on the other end of the line told me the coven accepted this. A feral pack softens when they believe you've given up.

After some mumbled and distant conversations that I couldn't quite make out, the line clicked, and I could tell the receiver had been picked up again.

"Listen, we appreciate that. And, just so you know, no one is trying to be aggressive or mean to you here. We all respect your role..."

For the record, that was a lie too. Here's the thing, narcissists are either gaslighting you or grooming you. You need to recognize the pattern to break it. It's like one of those, "What do you see? A witch or an old man?" quizzes in a magazine. You might have spent the entire relationship seeing the old man, until the *pattern* lets you see that it was a witch the entire time. That's life with a narcissist.

See their pattern once, and you'll see it always.

They continued, "It's just there's a brand table, and *we* control who sits at it. Got it?"

"Of course," I said.

The line went dead.

Entertainment is a minefield of mind games. In any board room you enter in this industry, and in others, I suppose, you'll find three certainties: Bottled water, greed, and ego. You can drown in all three.

Greed and ego are everywhere because they are the two main currencies of every narcissist. I've come to understand something about greed and ego. They're like a cold and a fever. One you feed and one you starve, if you hope to get the upper hand with either.

You feed a narcissist's ego, very carefully, just as you might an alligator. It's all they really care about. Compliments give them a sense of security. It distracts them so that you can simultaneously begin starving their emotional greed. You do *that* by not being entirely available to them, by not fully sharing.

It's a cat and mouse game that allows you to sustain a relationship with a narcissist — when you must — like a boss, coworker, or client.

If you're dating or married to a narcissist or if you have one as a parent, well, for that I'd have to quote the wise words of Carrie Underwood with "Jesus take the wheel."

Here's the truth: we *have* to protect our energy from the toxic people we encounter, and there will be many. Everything has a vibration. Us included. Spending time with people who strip us of ours, puts us more at risk for all the negative side effects that low frequency brings including anxiety, illness, sleeplessness, weight gain, all the outcomes we generally *don't* want.

I believe that if we protect one element in this life, it must be our energy. Greed and ego are the tides upon which narcissists sail, and honestly, they can have them. Energy is our current. It is what creates us, carries us, and connects us.

With regular humans we pursue social connections. With narcissists, we deploy strategy. Mine is a simple system. I created it in college in my senior advanced speech writing class. It's a technique meant to help candidates face an uncomfortable line of questions from a reporter or handle an adversary in a debate. It's a little song and dance I call P.M.P., not to be confused with Naughty by Nature's hit song, "O.P.P." Although both teach us something about people, don't they?

P.M.P. stands for Pause. Mirror. Pivot. If you've watched *Legally Blonde,* you might think of it as is my bend and snap.

The elevator pitch on P.M.P. is simple. People hate confrontation. It makes them feel out of control. That's because, for them, confrontation spins on an axis of emotions. For me, confrontation is not emotional. It's procedural.

In conflict, procedure is what keeps us ahead of our emotions. Think of it in terms of a soldier, firefighter, or

ER doctor; they rely on their training in a crisis. To put it simply, when the shit hits the fan, they don't fall apart. They fall back on what they have been taught.

For example, if you were in a home renovation accident, you would not want to arrive to the ER with a circular saw blade sticking out of your forehead to a doctor who takes one look at you, becomes hysterical, and says, "I don't need this today. I'm just not in a good place, okay?" before proceeding to cry in the hospital's supply closet.

No Ma'am. We want doctors who, even if for a millisecond have a mini freak out, that meltdown happens *internally,* as they simultaneously fly into action and save our lives as their training has taught them to do — preferably with a good plastic surgeon by their side. We have not been shellacking Hyaluronic Acid on our foreheads for a decade to end up with a scar from a saw. Please and thank you.

Procedure supports them as they navigate a tough situation, and it can support us, too.

First, we pause. We let the other person say all that he or she wants to say. We don't interrupt. We don't react. We are cool cucumbers, letting them get it all out. Maybe, we even actively listen. Nodding. Then, we take a breath. We think beyond the moment. Consider the big picture. Decide what we want the outcome of the communication to be. That is the trail we run down.

Then, we mirror.

Here's a fact: we all want to be seen and heard. It's hardwired into our reptile brains. It starts as a kid with, "Mom, look at me!" and unfolds from there.

Mirroring is reflecting back to what has been said or the state of the situation as it stands. It is a repeating back of the key portions of the conversation like, "I hear that you hate when I do that. I hear that it's been weighing on you..."

I'd like to note, that this does not mean forgiving, accepting, condoning, abetting, or anything of the sort. Nor does it mean reframing what they have said by imposing your take on it. That looks like this, "I hear you saying you hate when I do that, but that's because you're insecure." Hard no, unless you're ready to block punches.

Mirroring simply means echoing the circumstance in an unemotional way.

This ensures that everyone feels seen. In fact, most communications go south when someone believes he or she has not been "heard." Mirroring ensures this person knows you are paying attention to what he or she is saying *and* feeling.

Then, we pivot. This is where we redirect. This allows us to move toward an outcome that is better for us or de-escalates the situation. It also means we are now steering the conversation as opposed to being dragged behind the car.

Pivoting might look like this: "I know you felt undermined when I didn't back you up on no screen time for the kids. It wasn't my intention, but I see how you felt that. I also hear you saying that my overruling you, in front of them, trumped your authority. I do think we see screen time differently, but agree we need to be a united front. We have to find the common ground. What are you willing to give? I would say an hour a day is fair. Can you live with that?"

One critical element of P.M.P. is not responding to extreme declarative statements like, "You ALWAYS do this," or "You NEVER listen." Those are baited hooks. Every fish who bites that worm is then on the line, reeled in the direction of the person holding the pole. Resist the urge and swim past it.

Real talk, we need a strategy for toxic people because we don't really win, overcome, or change the behaviors of these individuals. Our goal is to avoid being pulled into their negative force field. What we want to do is immobilize them. P.M.P. is my course of action to do just that.

It's not easy. Protecting ourselves never is. By the time I called my mom on that Saturday morning, I had a junkyard full of narcissistic jalopies that I was actively and continually immobilizing. Six years straight, with no breaks. I was exhausted.

Then I started getting signs.

I'd come in from a walk with my dog, drenched from the pouring rain, to find a pristine white feather resting on the shoulder of my sopping wet raincoat.

I'd wake up in bed, roll over, and find a feather on my non-down pillow.

It began to happen more and more. Then I had the dream.

I called my mom back. "What if we went for Thanksgiving?"

"I'm already packed. I'll add my favorite pashmina to the bag."

Leave it to the one who raised me to know I'm a woman of action.

Three weeks later, we stepped out of our rental car and stood in front of The Inn of The Five Graces.

"You're early. Your room isn't ready quite yet. We'll get you lattes and you can wander the shops," the receptionist said as she directed a bell hop to collect our bags. "At the far end of the square you'll find local artists selling their wares. Start there. You can walk. You *should* walk. It's a gorgeous fall morning."

We set out just as encouraged, walking toward the town square. We window shopped along the way and marveled at the beauty of Santa Fe until finally we reached the far end of the town square where all the Native American artisans were gathered.

We'd only been there for a minute when I knelt down at that first woven blanket to look at a pile of handmade sterling silver rings. I smiled at the woman who sat perched in a camping chair keeping an eye over her wares.

"I think that man wants your attention."

I turned and stood as a man rushed toward me.

"I think this is the feather you were looking for," he said breathlessly, his face was full of anticipation for my response.

I looked down at his hands, calloused from decades of silversmithing, to find that he held a perfect, sterling silver feather cuff. He gestured for my arm. "May I?"

I extended my hand. He took it, and then he slipped the bracelet over my wrist.

I felt a piece of me, inside — that I hadn't even known was missing — slide into place with that feather. Fate has a way of finding the lost parts of us. I stared at the man with shining tears in my eyes. He looked both worried and supportive.

"I had a dream I came to Santa Fe for a feather," I said, biting my lower lip to keep it from trembling.

"Well, then you're right on time." He smiled. The warmth in his eyes reached my heart.

We both looked down with wonder at the feather.

"We believe a feather is a prayer in motion. I made this one a few weeks ago. It was meant to find its way to you," he said.

Toxic people, narcissists, and emotional vampires chip away at so many parts of us, and while P.M.P. and social awareness are important, so is this:

When we walk through life, holding ourselves in a protective stance to guard our energy and our heart from the toxic individuals around us, we sometimes lose sight of how powerful our energy really is when we unleash it. It's like a light on a dimmer. It has more power, but we've carefully, strategically set it at half — enough to light our path, not enough to inflame the ones in our lives who demand we shine less.

But we are not meant to shine less. We are meant to go all out at full wattage. People who can't handle that, don't deserve to put their hand on the dimmer.

So, while I want you and me to have a plan for the people who lessen our vibration, I do not want us to lower it ourselves. Quite the opposite, I want us to have authority over our own energy so that we can turn the wattage all the way up and handily deal with whoever has the audacity to touch the switch.

The man who made my feather bracelet mistook me for someone else, but not by mistake, by kismet. Despite all the narcissists, I kept my vibration and my personal power high. I always have. I always will.

The truth is what we look for is what we find. Patterns. People. Possibilities. Perceptions. Even bigger than that, though, is knowing that when we get really good at looking for what we want, we realize that if we also raise our vibration toward that dream, it will in turn look for us, too.

And feathers are just the start of what will float inside when we do.

SIX

The Cat Funeral

"P.S., I'm not going to your best friend's dead cat's funeral," Erin, my VP of everything at all moxie, said dryly from the passenger seat of our rental car.

We were in LA on business. Last minute meetings were to be expected. Feline calling hours were not.

"I guess you really don't want that promotion, then, do you?" I teased.

She smiled. Erin had worked for me for a decade, and, honestly, a cat memorial didn't even make it into the top ten weirdest things she'd seen in all those years. I didn't even have to look at her to know she was grimacing when Jules called.

"Mr. Whiskers had a stroke. It's time. Can you come?" Jules sobbed into the phone.

I looked at the clock on the car dash. We had four hours before our flight.

"Text me the address," I said.

"Thank you," her voice cracked, and the line went dead.

I redirected the car, crossing three lanes of the 405 to head in the other direction.

Fifteen minutes later we turned into the parking lot of the Met Pet Animal Clinic.

"Just so we're clear, I'm staying in the car," Erin said as I spiraled up the ramp of the parking garage.

"See what a good boss I am?" I said dramatically as I pulled into a spot on the roof. "Look at that view." LA unfolded before us.

"Just what I always wanted, a corner office at a cat funeral," Erin said sweetly.

I laughed as I started to get out.

"Text me when it gets weird," she said as she cracked open her laptop to work.

"We're putting her cat down, Erin. I don't think there'll be much room for weird."

"We'll see," she warned.

Now, as I sat in the exam room, Erin's warning ringing in my ears, I realized she was right. I was in an episode of *Curb Your Enthusiasm.*

"That's not my wallet," Jules said, pulling me back to the room.

"What?" I asked, confused as I looked down at the pouch in my hands and the contents of the purse strewn across my lap. "Why is there someone else's bag in your room?" I questioned, realizing I had just rifled through a stranger's purse.

When Jules didn't answer, I looked up to see her carefully scooping a dollop of cat food onto a tongue depressor before holding it in front of Mr. Whiskers.

I put the wallet down and walked over to her, putting my arm around her.

"He isn't eating. Do you think they have another flavor?" she asked, her eyes pooling with tears.

I ushered her to the row of plastic seats that sat bolted to the wall of the exam room.

"I don't think he *needs* a different flavor," I said softly.

"What if he's hungry? He should have a last meal."

"That's for convicted criminals. Cats, not so much," I rationalized delicately. "Besides, aren't we," I paused, searching for a palatable way to say it, "*ending* him soon?"

Her lip trembled. "We have a lot to do before that can happen," she said.

Confusion clouded my brow, "What do you mean, a lot to do?"

Before she could answer, the door to the room banged open, and a vet tech struggled to fit through the doorway with four metal chairs. With each step she took, their metal frames clanged together loudly. Jules and I winced. Mr. Whiskers looked dead to the world. *Oh God, is he dead,* I thought, slightly panicking, even though that was, clearly, the whole point of us being there.

"Is this gonna be enough chairs?" the tech asked, opening them.

"Are there more?" Jules asked.

More? I thought.

"Not really," the vet tech said with a shrug.

"Well then, I guess it'll have to work."

I stared at Jules in disbelief. *How many chairs do you need to put a cat down?* I thought.

When the tech left, I asked, "Why do we need more chairs?"

I waited for her reply. She was busy making a second attempt at spoon-feeding her paralyzed cat.

"They're for everyone who's coming."

I accepted this answer. That happens with crazy. It can lap itself and land back at normal. It doesn't sound possible, but have you ever been to a cat's funeral?

"And the wallet?"

"That's Jenny's. She left right before you got here to get the neighbor's dogs and Hunnah and Halloween." *Jules's dog and other cat.*

"The *neighbor's* dogs are coming?"

"They love Mr. Whiskers," Jules said earnestly.

The door to the room opened, and the veterinarian walked in. "How are we doing in here?"

Jules pouted out her bottom lip as a response, fighting back tears. My heart broke for her.

"We're ready anytime you are," he consoled, putting his arm around her.

"I just need more time so everyone can say good-bye."

The vet nodded. "I've got some oxygen for Mr. Whiskers. We'll keep him propped up until you're ready."

I watched, then, as the veterinarian laid a tube with a funnel on the end near Mr. Whiskers. Have you ever bit your tongue so hard that it's actually a Kegel? Because I was kind of there.

As I watched the vet carefully adjust the feline oxygen tube, two men swanned in.

"Julllleeesss," the new arrivals crooned, immediately embracing her.

As they hugged, the door swung back open again, and a woman with three dogs and a cat entered. *Ah, this must be Jenny,* I thought. Without introduction or hesitation, the woman shoved the leashes into my hand and dropped the cat into my arms before joining the group's hug. All of them were openly crying as I juggled a menagerie of confused pets all by myself.

One of the dogs looked at me like, "fucking humans," and you know what? He *or she* was right.

When the group of mourners broke apart, one of the men came over to me.

"How are *you* holding up?" he soothed. He wore a medical grade face mask with a bandana tied over top of it and gloves on his hands. Mind you, this was years before COVID.

"I'm good. But, are you okay?" I asked, gesturing toward his protective gear.

"Oh, yes. I'm just deathly allergic to cats." He pulled a package of Clorox bleach wipes from his pocket to sanitize his seat. "Deathly," he stressed as he sat down.

Oh Lord, I hope we don't have to put him down, too, I thought.

As I juggled my pack of animals, I watched this man register the fact that his perfectly pressed chinos and Ralph Lauren shirt now had cat hair all over them. He stood back up and pulled a travel lint roller from his other pocket. Carefully, he peeled off the outer layer.

"Just gonna lint roll all this cat hair off of me. It's like a magnet, isn't it?" he said, worry at the edges of his voice. "Don't want to take it with me and die on the ride home, do I?" he offered with grim sarcasm.

"Definitely not," I agreed as I watched him discard three peels of adhesive before nervously resuming his wipe down of the remaining folding chairs in the room.

I looked at my watch. I had been there for nearly two hours. I had to go. I had to get to the airport. I stood to make my exit just as Jules began the phone tree portion of the day. She dialed and then placed the speakerphone right next to Mr. Whiskers who sat stoically on the metal exam table, his nose near the oxygen funnel, not listening.

First a niece was called, then a nephew. After that, Jules rang her father, who sounded like Jimmy Stewart in *It's a Wonderful Life*. He crooned over the line, "Mr. Whiskers you were a goooooooood caaaaat."

A sudden cackling laugh filled the room. I was shocked because it had burst forward from *me* before I could stop it. Every person *and* animal in the room, of which there were nine I might add, turned to look me.

Jules's face crumpled with sadness, so I did what had to be done. I pretended I was sobbing.

Allergy man fled to my side. I let him console me.

Shortly thereafter, I departed. I felt bad for leaving, mostly because Mr. Whiskers looked like he was counting on me to the be the only sane one in the room willing to pull the plug, but I had a plane to catch and a vodka tonic to purchase to help me walk off the events of the past two and half hours.

When I got into the car, Erin asked, "And?"

"He's still alive," I groaned.

"How?" she asked shocked. "You were in there for two and half hours."

"Turns out Mr. Whiskers has a lot of friends to call."

She stared at me blankly. "I told you it would get weird," she said.

Halfway home to Chicago, just after the beverage cart had gone by, the text arrived. I read it and then handed my phone across the aisle to Erin so she could read it, too.

It is with a broken heart that I write to tell you that I have just said goodbye to my beloved Mr. Whiskers. He has left us much, much too soon...

After reading, Erin handed my phone back to me.

"I'm guessing Mr. Whiskers would have liked it to happen *just* a little bit sooner," I said.

"Ya think?" Erin offered.

Here's the thing about the funeral of Mr. Whiskers. It is proof of something very important that I've come to understand about human behavior. Everyone has a process. Not all processes are good. Not all are healthy. And, half the time our chosen process becomes a crutch that only delays our expansion. Yet we cling to the process we have come to know.

And, yes we can go around trying to impose *our* way on one another. We can become frustrated when others won't or don't follow the plan *we* think is best. We can steamroll each other and make comments like, "It's my way or the highway." We can even try and shame one another into action.

Some of that *will* work. Some of those have to work. Not every situation we enter into is a democratic one. As my mom used to remind us, "Oh, I'm sorry; did I give you the impression that this was a democracy? My bad. It's not."

Having said that, leadership is a team sport. Yes, being a boss or head of a household *can* mean that we're telling people what to do, laying down the law and demanding results. That might look like a mom who has blown her stack, yet again, after finding towels on the bathroom floor for the umpteenth time and decrees, "Pick up your towels or else!"

She's not a woman asking for accountability; she is instilling it.

There is plenty of *that* in leadership, but there is also this: Make room for the lived experiences of those who sit at your table.

Children. Friends. Employees. Spouses. Each of us is, certainly, having a different lived experience. Even if we are siblings raised in the same house. Even if we are doing the same job for the same pay for the same number of years. Even if we are parenting all the children the same way.

No matter what. No matter who. We are all internalizing the world around us differently, and we bring those internalized observations with us everywhere we go. It's the data by which we make sense of the world. Some of it is bad data, but that doesn't change that it's a key part of us, and it informs so much of our behavior.

A healthy process is an essential part of our effectiveness. An unhealthy process is a billboard for our inefficiencies. Know which side of the street you live on. Know which side of the street your friends, family, or spouse — really anyone bringing energy your way — lives on, too.

When we meet people, when we join a team — be it for work, life, or for love —we arrive and say, "Here's what I bring to the table...." Then we fill in the blank of that statement with a skill, asset, or attribute. What almost always goes unsaid is the process by which our talent unfolds.

When I started hiring people, looking for the talents that would round out my team, I realized that if I wanted these new hires to show up and share their craft, be it a designer, photographer, or videographer, I needed to make room for their process to unfold, either in part or in whole.

In essence, people often need two seats at the table. One for them and one for the process by which they bring that capability to life.

This is not to say that we should condone unhealthy practices. But, not making room for their practice while simultaneously expecting the highest output from them is a recipe for frustration, anger, resentment, and all the other things we find on the salad bar of "I hate this place."

And, it doesn't mean that we won't eventually shift, mold, and shape their process. We will. Healthy relationships and discourse always stretch, inform, and challenge our approach.

It's why experience is everything. It's why failure is good. It's why jumping into the deep end, even if we can't see the bottom, is necessary from time to time.

When we do, our process benefits from the new data we receive.

Jules was in her process. I may not have fully understood it. It may not have been the way I would have gone about it, but it was what she needed to make sense of her impending loss. To be critical of it in the moment would have expanded her pain. My job as her friend was to be the balm to her wound, not to impose upon her how I thought she should heal it.

When we allow people their process, we afford them their peace.

Mr. Whiskers was my reminder of that. He was, also, my reminder to be very clear on who I want pulling my plug, should it ever come to that. I don't think anyone will be surprised to learn it's not going to be Jules, except maybe Jules. It's just that A *Weekend at Bernie's* style trip to Palm Springs for a post-mortem good-bye is not exactly how I'd like to kick off my stairway to heaven, if you know what I mean.

SEVEN

Orgies in the Park

"Merna," I hissed, desperate to get her attention.

She didn't turn around. She stood 25 feet from me, tail wagging, staring up at three naked people in Central Park.

"Get over here right now," I said through gritted teeth.

She looked back at me, cocked her head to the side, and ignored me completely before outright defying my command and moving closer to the group. It was 7:10 a.m. on a Sunday morning. In the distance I could hear a lakeside church service happening, but I had to focus really hard to hear the pastor over the grunting and moaning of the trio before me.

"You are a traitor, Merna," I accused, looking around, desperate, for an alternate plan, one that did not include me walking into an orgy to get my dog.

"I will leave you here," I said defiantly.

As if testing my empty threat, she sat down right where she stood, which just happened to be directly beside the ass of one of the naked men.

Shit. I thought.

I had rescued Merna in Chicago. My mom and family reminded me regularly that I had no business getting a dog. I traveled weekly for my company and worked 70 plus hour weeks. In their opinion I was being selfish to want a pet. But then my friend Lesley chimed in and said, "I think if you're too busy for a dog, then you're too busy for a life. I don't like that for you. You should have a life. Get the dog."

On the heels of Lesley's affirmation, I told my mom the search was on. I could feel her roll her eyes through the phone.

When my mother came to Chicago a month later to visit, I dragged her to an adoption event and two shelters in search of my future pet.

Then, as if proving my mother right, I got called out of town during her stay. Her mother daughter trip to Chicago was suddenly minus her daughter.

"*See*, what would you have done, if you had a dog?" she pointed out righteously, as she dropped me at O'Hare airport.

"I'd make you watch it," I said with a wave as I headed in to catch my flight to LA for a three-day shoot.

On the day before my return, my mom called and asked, "What's with all this canned cat food by the door? I keep tripping over it."

I had a cat at the time, Jersey. She was demanding and stand-offish, but like all other cat parents I did her bidding in the hopes of getting a morsel of love every now and again.

"It's Jersey's," I answered. "Ten years eating the same special cat food for her bladder, and she's suddenly decided she hates it. I had to get her a new kind. The vet wouldn't take those cans back. I need to donate them. There's, like, twenty cans left in that box."

"Where were planning to take them?" my mom asked.

"I don't know. I haven't researched. Maybe the shelter downtown."

"Okay," she said.

"Okay, what?"

"Okay, I'll take it tomorrow before you get back."

I was shocked. My mom had always been the sort to avoid upsetting animal encounters. If we saw a box of puppies for adoption at the entrance to the IGA, she'd shove us past before we could pet them. "We can't rescue them all," she'd chide. It always struck me as odd because forget rescuing them *all,* we'd never even rescued *one.* We never had a dog.

Yet, here she was, offering to walk into the lion's den of this shelter. I was even more shocked when the next day she announced this bulletin, "I found your dog."

"What?" I said, stopping abruptly in the taxi line at O'Hare, the person behind me running into the back of me with a move already glare.

I waved the man past so I could hear my mother better.

"I dropped off the food like you said, and I stayed to play with the cats. Then I went in and saw the dogs. The second I laid eyes on him, I said to myself, 'That's Kristin's dog.' He's super cute with wiry fur and big soulful eyes. Kinda like Benji."

This was not the ostrich behavior I was used to.

"Stay there, I'm coming," I said.

"What? I already left."

"Well, go back," I directed as I threw my suitcase into the trunk of a taxi.

Twenty minutes later, I was standing at the front desk of the Anti-Cruelty Society of Chicago.

"My mom just dropped off some cat food. She said she saw a dog she thought I should meet. He's wiry. Mid-sized."

The woman disappeared into the back and came out with the exact dog I had described, except he was so hyper and barky, I couldn't even pet him.

"I don't think she meant this dog. I feel like my mom said he was like Benji. Light brown. This dog's grey."

The woman thought for a second. "Well, we don't have a *he* that's brown, but we have a *she*."

"Maybe," I said, optimistically.

She swept the energetic Petey away as I sat on the bench to wait.

A second later she returned with a timid and quaking, blonde mutt.

"Her name's Fawn," the shelter worker said.

Fawn walked right up to me, stared into my eyes, and then buried her forehead into my knees. She shook like a leaf.

I lifted her chin so that I could look at her, and I burst into tears. *This was my dog.*

"That's the one," my mom said breathlessly as she rushed towards us. "Right?" she prompted.

I nodded. "I want to adopt her," I said smiling at the worker through my tears.

"That's great, but we don't do adoptions after 5:30 p.m. You'll have to come back tomorrow."

I felt a stab in my heart at the thought of leaving this dog one more night in the shelter. "Are you sure? Can't we just get it done fast?"

"Unfortunately, no," she apologized. "Tell you what, why don't you help me put her back in her kennel, and tomorrow she's yours."

I wiped my tears away and followed her into the back. The already-kenneled dogs started barking at the sight of us. Fawn recoiled on her leash, desperate for the lobby and the freedom of the street outside.

"It's okay. It's just one more night," I promised, as I watched the woman latch the metal gate of Fawn's crate.

As the employee and I stood talking about the materials I would need for the impending adoption, another staffer came in with a clipboard in hand and began moving the dogs from crate to crate. Fawn was one of the dogs the worker moved. I watched as the employee then took a red wax pen from the wall and drew a line through the crate tags of the five dogs he had positioned into a singular row of kennels by the staff only door.

"Are you marking her because you know I'm adopting her?" I asked.

He spun to face me. "What? You're adopting her?" He looked panicked.

"Yea, they told me I couldn't take her today. I have to come back tomorrow."

His face grew serious. "You have to come first thing. Go to the back door. The employee door. Tell them you want a redline dog. Do you hear me?"

I realized as he spoke that Fawn was literally on death row. She was going to be put down in the morning, along with the four other dogs bookending her, Petey being one of them.

"Are you euthanizing her?" I asked, terrified.

"Not if you come to the back door. Be here half an hour before we open. Got it?"

I nodded and looked down at Fawn. *My dog.* She was trembling in fear. So was I. I turned around, took his red pen, scratched out the name Fawn, and wrote in Merna. I had no idea where the name came from, but it appeared in my brain and, I felt like they might not kill her if they knew someone had named her.

"I'm your governor's call. I'll be here at 8 a.m. I promise." Then I cried all the way home for Petey.

Seven years and one cross country move later, Merna now sat 20 feet from me watching an *Indecent Proposal* in Central Park.

"You are a turncoat, Merna Rose," I hissed, walking toward her *and* the three homeless people openly having sex at sunrise. Here, I haven't even gone ice skating yet in Central Park and already I'm at an orgy. This city has so much to offer.

One of the men saw me advancing and placed his hands on his hips and swung his erect penis in a circle like a cabaret dancer would the tassels on her set of pasties.

"Thank you, but no, sir," I said. I am nothing if not polite, even at an orgy, it turns out. It's definitely the Midwesterner in me.

Merna, of course, saw me coming and jumped up. The second man strained to reach for Merna. Seeing as he was *attached* to another human, I got to her first.

I grabbed Merna, placed her on her lead, and pulled her down the path as I heard the woman begin to yell, "Faster. Faster!"

I don't know if the two men listened, but I sure did. Merna and I broke out into a full run.

Out of all the advice I got before officially moving to NYC, no one cautioned me about the area of the park that we were in, The Ramble. In case you don't know, The Ramble is a 36-acre plot of woodland grounds located in the heart of Central Park, falling between 73rd and 79th Streets.

It's majestic and transports you from Manhattan's urban jungle to the beautiful landscapes more commonly found in upstate New York. It is known for its excellent bird watching and, as I learned firsthand, public sex acts. So, when an ornithologist in the park inquires, "Is that a Dickcissel?" You'll have to ask what kind of pecker the birdwatcher is seeing through his or her binoculars to be sure.

I knew none of this, of course, and for the first three months after our move, Merna and I spent every weekend in The Ramble hiking through all 36acres. We developed a routine. Each day we went to the park. Dogs are allowed off leash before 9 a.m., so we went early. Monday through Friday, we stayed just inside the park entrance by my apartment. On the weekends, we hit up the whole park, walking for hours. It was our Shangri-La.

In fact, The Ramble was one of my favorite discoveries. If you've been, then you know I was breaking the law by allowing Merna off leash. The Ramble is one of the areas of the park that has posted and enforced leash laws, a rule we typically followed. That morning, however, as Merna pulled repeatedly on the leash to chase birds, I spilled my coffee twice. I decided *how much harm could it do to let her off leash one time?*

I think we all have our answer.

I stopped going to The Ramble after that morning. Looking back now, I realize I wish I hadn't. Arguably it was a traumatic scene, but the part of me that yearned for nature's wild places, loved that patch of woods in the middle of the city's cement.

Instead, I did what we so diligently do with trauma; I put up the no trespassing sign and moved on. Forget it. Unhabitable land.

But trauma is like a forest. We can brick it up, but that doesn't stop it from growing. It's just that now it's behind a wall where we can't tame it. In our absence...or maybe better stated, in our avoidance....it becomes prolific by its own accord; its tentacles climb up and over the walls and grab for other lands not intended for it like our relationships, mindsets, and priorities.

We ask ourselves, "Why is nothing I'm doing working? Why am I so anxious? Why do all of my relationships fall apart this way?" We beat ourselves up, furious, forgetting that the entire time there's a world of explanation behind that boarded-up wall within.

Here's the crux, hang all the KEEP OUT signs you want. Trauma doesn't read. Like dandelions and poison oak, it's invasive. It hangs on. It's a part of our human geography, really. We don't have to see the earth's tectonic plates to know that they made the mountains. Same goes for our trauma. Pain pressing into the topography of our lives, whether we have awareness of it or not.

I think walling up what has hurt us only encourages it to become more wild.

Did we learn nothing from *Nell,* aside from the fact that not even actress and icon Jodie Foster can overcome a questionable script? As a plot line, someone left Nell alone in the woods. I want to say she was raised by wolves. Regardless, she returned feral, with a language all her own.

How can we not expect the same from our trauma?

Left to its own devices, what hurt us finds its own language in the form of addiction, inability to commit, intimacy issues, anxiety, food control, or a hundred other things.

We then spend years battling the language of our pain. But I have to wonder, wouldn't it be better to reclaim the land that trauma took and give it our *own* language? Decide what our trauma means to us instead of letting it dictate the direction of its meaning?

It's not a theory I hatched entirely on my own. After I experienced the following sudden and difficult loss, a friend of mine shared some advice that changed me forever.

On December 26, 2004, I woke up on the sofa of my parent's home in Ohio over my holiday break. I had fallen asleep with the Christmas tree lights still on. I don't recall why the channel was tuned to CNN. I had drifted off watching a Hallmark movie.

But, these words gripped me in my slumber, "A tsunami has struck the Indian Ocean. Details are just now coming in, but tens of thousands are feared dead with thousands more missing."

Hearing those words I sat bolt upright, instantly groping for my glasses in the dark so that I could see the screen.

The reporter continued, "A 9.1 magnitude earthquake struck the region which triggered a tsunami. Many of us here in studio had never heard that word," the reporter explained. "A tsunami is a displacement of a large volume of water, in this case caused by an earthquake or eruption that resulted in the sea floor suddenly rising up or lowering down. The water is then displaced, pulled far out to sea so that the seafloor is entirely exposed. But within minutes all that water pushes right back toward the shoreline with tremendous force, we're talking waves a hundred feet tall."

Giving up on my glasses, I flung myself directly in front of the television. The footage I saw was terrifying. I watched in horror as massive waves filled with cars, trees, boats, and buildings tore into the shores of Sri Lanka, destroying everything in their path. I began to sob.

Two people who were very dear to me were vacationing in that region, in that exact bay as a matter of fact. My heart thundered with a terrifying awareness that they might now *no longer* be alive.

My parents, still in bed, heard me, and came out to the living room. Groggily they appeared in the doorway, "What's wrong?" my mother asked, worriedly.

"Where's my phone?" I asked ignoring her, spinning from the television to begin my second search of the morning.

"What's happening?" my mom asked again, her concern growing at the sight of my hysteria.

"I plugged it in at some point. Can one of you *please* help me find it?" I shouted at them.

"Okay," my dad said as he and mother began to search with me, shaking out the blankets, both of them suppressing their confusion over my behavior.

"Tell us what's going on," my mom encouraged.

"These your glasses?" my dad asked.

I snatched my frames from him and walked into the kitchen extending the search for my phone into the other rooms of the house. I could feel a panic rising in my chest.

I spied my phone plugged into an outlet behind a stack of Christmas cookie tins and ripped it from the wall. I punched the *on* button.

The screen illuminated and seventeen voicemails flooded in. It was only 7 a.m. on the day after Christmas.

While my parents continued searching for the phone that was now in my hand, I became laser focused on my messages. I hit play.

"Kristin, call me. It's Lis. Is he there? Isn't that exactly where they went on vacation?"

"Hey, K, I think something's happened in Sri Lanka. Call me. NOW."

I listened to each message, but only for as long as it took for me to assess if the caller had information to share or was just asking the same questions that I had. If they didn't have new information, I moved past them to the next message.

They were a mix of producers, friends, and colleagues.

My chest tightened with each one. My parents were now zeroed in on the newsfeed on CNN. Comprehension flooded their faces. They knew that my longtime client and his beloved partner were in Sri Lanka. I had represented this particular person for so long that our relationship at the time was as much talent and manager as it was family.

The phone messages in my ear continued. "*K, call me. Have you heard anything?*"

Next.

"*Kristin, are you seeing this? I'm freaking out at the news reports.*"

And then, I heard the voice of my client's mother. "K, it's me. He called me. He's alive. He's okay, but Fernando is missing. I don't know what to do or how to get him. Call me as soon as you get this."

That's when my knees gave out. I buckled to the floor. I began to wail, only I didn't know I was crying. My mother told me later, "It looked like you were some sort of wounded animal. It was terrifying."

My whole life, I've heard the phrase *it brought me to my knees*. In that moment I knew exactly what it meant.

To have people you love a world away, hurt, lost, and missing... To be filled with *relief* at learning that one has miraculously survived and the other is devastatingly missing... It was wrenching.

I had no time to process any of that. I was immediately on the phone and organizing with news outlets the possibility of a trade: a live report in return for a rescue helicopter being sent to the region where we believed my client and a group of other survivors were trapped.

The days that followed were filled with returning dozens of calls to media outlets, fending off interviews, and hiring a private search and rescue team in the hopes of finding our still missing loved one.

I learned things about ground searches and morgue mapping that shattered my heart in ways I can't explain.

I didn't eat. I didn't sleep. I worked 16hr days. My phone rang incessantly, and tabloid reporters pounded on my door at 4 a.m. looking for quotes.

I felt like I was doing everything I could and yet nothing that mattered, because Fernando was still missing.

Within days, the world knew that hundreds of thousands were dead. The weeks ahead would reveal that Fernando was gone, too.

It was during that time that a girlfriend of mine called to check in on me.

"How are you doing? And don't just say fine. No one's fine right now."

"Well, it's not great," I said, my voice wavering, "but clearly this isn't about me."

She paused. "No, but I'm going to tell you something anyway. It's not *now* information. It's future information, okay?"

"Okay," I agreed.

"At some point, you're going to get to decide what all this means. This loss. This sadness. Life isn't defined for us. It's defined by us. We pick the meaning. Even if we decide, today it's all fucked' tomorrow we can decide differently. Each *day* we decide...each *minute* if that's what it takes. Okay?"

I began to weep for my friend who had lived and my friend who had died.

Pain is real, but that doesn't mean it won't bend under the weight of the perception we place upon it.

We can spend decades trying to learn the words our pain wants us to use and wake up tomorrow and flip the script by giving our trauma an entirely different language, one of our own making.

I can't help but think about the tsunami. I think about what it was to wake up drowning, beds and nightstands floating on the ceiling, water pinning people underneath.

I think about my friend.

Fernando didn't come home, but we can, even to the hardest parts of us.

EIGHT

Hold on to Your Nipples

"Go left!" I shrieked.

"I can't!" my dad snarled back.

"What do you mean you can't?! You're the one steering," I screamed. I began digging my paddle into the water, desperately trying to work against the rapids.

"I'm not steering. I'm the power," my dad corrected.

"What?" I swung to face him, my legs burning on the hot aluminum of my seat. "Are you crazy? The person in the back of the canoe always steers. *I'm* the power! I'm in the front."

My dad stared at me. "Oh," he said.

"Do you even know how to canoe?" I accused. I faced forward again. "You have to steer us left!" I demanded, attempting to help him by paddling against the current.

Following my lead, my dad joined in. We were both furiously backpaddling now.

"Shit," my dad said. I looked at him. He nodded ahead.

I spun to see our fate. It was a mere 30 yards away, and we were being pulled toward it. I clutched the sides of our canoe in terror and began to scream.

It was the summer of 1987. I was twelve years old. My dad had, once again, offered to take us canoeing. There were three boats on the river that day. My brother, Brian, and some neighbor boys had commandeered the other two. My dad and I were in the last canoe, bringing up the rear.

I had only agreed to go on the trip because my mom had put the fear of God, Jesus, and Mary into my father before we left.

"You will not, under any circumstance, have a repeat of last year. Do you understand me?" my mom threatened him.

"I'm not a kid, Janet," my dad said as he spread ketchup on Wonder Bread in our small kitchen.

My mom snorted aggressively. "I'll just say this. If you kill our children, I will kill you."

Three hours later as I sat at the bow of our canoe watching our fate close in on us, I shouted at the top of my lungs, "Mom's gonna kill you!"

"I knoooowww!" my dad cried back.

The year before, our semi-annual neighborhood canoeing trip had been a doozy, hence my mom's "I Know What You Did Last Summer" warning. My father was legendary in our neighborhood for being the one brave parent to take us on group outings. Canoeing. Concerts. Cedar Point. My dad was an icon.

The word was out. Our canoe trip was on. The troops were to gather in our yard at 7 a.m. on Saturday. My cousin decided she would join us. To this day, my aunt, her mother, cannot hear of our '86 canoe trip without glaring at my father and reminding him, "I'm still mad at you about it."

Family lore says my aunt was so furious that even as a lifelong pacificist, she had punched my dad right in the gut when we got home, and she learned what had happened.

That day, like this one, had started as planned. Bologna sandwiches were made, cans of pop were packed, and the boombox was loaded into the van. At seven on the dot, we piled in and were off, a merry band of neighbors in swim trunks and terry cloth rompers.

We arrived ready for the river. The canoe livery employees loaded us into their beat-up, old bus to drive us a couple of miles upriver. There we would be dropped off, and our boats would be placed on the water. On the drive, we had been warned of water moccasins and sunburns. It was the 80s, so we were afraid of *only* one of those two.

At the boat launch, we sorted ourselves into pairs and hopped into canoes. Down the river we went. Laughing. Chatting. Splashing. Two snake sightings, one rolled canoe, a missing bottle of Avon's Skin So Soft — our bug spray — and a stop for lunch later, we came upon a group of people climbing up and jumping off a truss bridge.

We floated below them on the water, heads back, watching in awe as they leapt. We marveled at their bravery.

"Think we could handle it?" my dad cajoled.

Given how many boys were with us, it felt like he was putting a heat lamp on a powder keg. I could tell they were biting at the bit to try it for themselves.

"Should we?" one asked.

"We're here," another answered with a shrug.

"I mean, it must be okay if they're doing it," the others observed.

Before I could protest, our entire crew was in the water, pulling the boats ashore and clamoring up the rocks to the bridge.

"Come on. It's not that tall. You can handle it. Don't be a baby," my dad said, pushing me along the jagged path everyone had followed to the top.

I was terrified, but I allowed myself to be shoved forward. The first observation I made was that, from below, the bridge had looked tall but not *high*. From the top I realized it was as tall as standing on the roof of our house.

My stomach tied in knots.

One by one, I watched in horror as each member of our group climbed up and over the rail to jump, including my cousin, hence my aunt's continued resentment on the topic.

As each person leapt, I clutched the rail more tightly. My dad offered his hand to hoist me over to the outer edge.

I gingerly climbed over. Everyone cheered.

Pee ran down my legs.

"Is the bridge swaying?" my brother asked, now back for his second jump.

"It's your sister," someone said.

I looked down at my knees to find them shaking so violently that the entire end of the bridge where I stood was vibrating.

"You're such a wimp," my brother said with a laugh, hovering above me, as he stood atop the rail. Then poof, he was gone.

It was just my father and I on the bridge now.

I looked down. Six heads bobbed in the water below us, splashing and laughing. "Come on, jump," they shouted up at me.

If I could have, I would have peed more.

"I can't do it," I said to my dad, beginning to turn around.

"How are you going to get down if you don't jump?"

I was attempting to crawl back over to the road side of the bridge, when my dad swung his leg over the rail to join me.

"I'll climb down," I reasoned.

"How? It's too steep. At least here," he said pointing down to the muddy river below, "you'll hit the water. If you climb back down those rocks, you'll break your arm."

"As opposed to my neck?" I accused, gesturing to murky water below, before clinging back to the truss of the bridge.

"You won't break your neck," he chided. "You just have to hit the water right."

"Hit the water *right*?" I questioned. "You're making this worse."

"You gotta do it," my dad encouraged. "I'll go, and you follow, okay?"

Apparently, it was a rhetorical question, because before I could answer, he leapt.

I heard the splash before my brain could process that he had jumped. I was now alone on the bridge. The last idiot standing. I stared down at him. *To betray your own daughter,* I thought.

"You gotta do it!" he yelled, his hands circling his mouth so I could hear his lone shout.

"I can't!" I yelled back.

"You can!" my dad, brother, and two neighbor kids shouted up in unison.

"What if there's a giant rock or a huge tree under the water? I'll kill myself!" I reasoned back.

"Whatever," my brother shouted, but I could tell by my father's face that this was the first time he had considered *that* as a possibility.

"Jump right where I did. It's a safe spot," my dad instructed, sounding less confident than he had a minute before.

Tired of waiting for me, my brother, the guys, and my cousin began to board their canoes. My dad watched them, worriedly, as they began to paddle off. Despite his now obvious breach in credibility, he remained our lone chaperone and, thus, needed to follow them.

"We gotta stay together, Kristin. Jump!" he yelled, watching their boats disappear around the bend.

"You're pressuring me!" I screamed, my voice cracking with terror.

"Okaaaay. OK," he allowed, "Take your time." Less than two seconds later, though, when I hadn't moved, he shouted, "Seriously!"

My mom had always asked us, "If your friends jumped off a bridge, would you?" Our answer was always, "No. Duh." She never asked, though, "If your *dad* jumped off a bridge, would you?"

This was unchartered territory.

"KRISTIN!" he bellowed again.

Well mom, here's your answer, I thought. The others had *jumped.* I would say that mine was less a leap and more a falling forward.

Of course, I hit the water like a seal flopping on a dock, became disoriented, and started to sink. My dad had to search the murky depth and pull me up. He then dragged me to the canoe as I coughed up water. I was white as a sheet. I could feel it.

He hoisted me inside like someone pushing a heavy suitcase up into the overhead bin. Awkward. Labored. He then pulled himself in and began paddling like mad to catch up to my brother. I don't remember much after that point, except for the conversation in the car on the ride home.

"Let *me* tell your mom and Phyl about the bridge, okay?" my dad had instructed.

My cousin, my brother, and I had all nodded in unison, frankly relieved that my dad would be in striking distance instead of us.

"And, when they ask how tall the bridge was, what's your answer?"

He had directed the question to all of three of us, but I noticed, he'd only turned to look at me.

"Not very tall," my brother and cousin said. I, however, didn't answer.

My dad held my gaze in the rearview mirror. I think he knew, right then, that he was screwed. I was, at best, the weak link in his cover story. At worst, the whistleblower.

So, when *this* year's canoe trip came around, my mom had been very clear. "NO jumping off bridges, trees, tall rocks, nothing. You stay in your canoes." We all nodded yes. "And you keep your life vests on."

"Janet, don't be ridiculous. It's the Mohican River. You can stand up in it," my dad argued back.

"Funny last year it was deep enough to jump off a 25-foot bridge," my mom said crossing her arms and glaring at him.

Yet, despite my mom's explicit directions, my dad and I were installed in our canoe preparing to drown, not a life vest on either one of us.

We had been warned, of course, of this impending doom. All day, as we made our way down the river, our lead canoes had shouted back instructions. "Lunch spot ahead." "Go right!" Our last instruction was "STAY LEFT!" We knew it had to be a big one because, while all the other instructions had been shouted back just once, this warning had been yelled four times.

I parroted each directive to my father. He was our stern man. If you don't know, which clearly my father didn't, the stern is the back of the boat, and the person seated there is responsible for steering.

As we came around the bend, we saw it, a giant fallen oak. It was massive and lay across the riverbed. I gasped.

The map of the river ahead was this: In the middle of the river was an island. To the left, still waters. To the right, fast flowing rapids that rushed under the oak, its humongous trunk blocking passage.

"Steer left!" I shouted immediately. But like a car in a fishtail, my dad steered right. "Nooooooo!" I screamed.

The current began to work against us, pulling us closer to the right.

"Shit! What do we do?" my grown-ass father asked me, his twelve-year-old daughter.

I looked around for our options, which were slim.

"The island! We'll pull our canoe across!" I directed.

We paddled for our lives toward the narrow sliver of land, but it was no use. We were no match for the current. It pulled us right, and as we paddled, we spun, momentarily facing our boat upstream and headed backwards toward our impending doom. We screamed like two small children on a haunted house ride, aggressively paddling until we spun back around.

In the distance I could hear my brother and the neighbor boys shouting, "BAIL OUT! BAIL OUT NOW!"

We ricocheted off a boulder to the other side of the river. Desperate, my father reached up and grabbed the branches that hung overhead from the trees along the banks. It was an attempt to slow us down. It didn't work. The force of the water was carrying us too quickly, and the branches just pulled from his grip, leaving a sort of rope burn up his arms, the leaves lashing him. As each branch escaped his grip, he let out a sort of gurgled scream of pain.

"Daaaaaddddd! Do something," I shrieked as we closed in on the massive oak.

"Like what?" he shouted passive-aggressively.

Then I spotted it. Water was flowing under a portion of the trunk that had been narrowed due a lost limb.

"LEFT!" I shouted, pointing at the spot.

Without even questioning me, my dad began wildly paddling to the left. The two of us getting under that tree would be like watching a bear squeeze through a cat door, but it was the only Hail, Mary we had, so I dug in right alongside him, paddling like an Olympic-level kayaker fighting for the gold.

For just a moment, hope swelled. But then I saw just how preposterously small the opening was. I knew in that instant it wasn't possible. Even if the boat could fit under, I didn't see how we could.

Having missed our shot to bail, I had one option left. I slid backward off my seat, and lay down in the bottom of the canoe, letting my dad take an entire oak tree on the chin.

"What are you doing?" he asked, terrified, as I shoved our life vests out of the way, wedging myself into the bottom of the boat.

"Sorry," I shouted.

I watched his face briefly register what was about to happen just before we were in the branches. Limbs smacked my legs as the metal of our boat screeched around me. We violently listed sideways. Water poured in over the edges of the canoe. I clung to both life vests.

I couldn't see my father and wouldn't have even known if he was in the boat were it not for his high-pitched screams.

When we came out the other side, the canoe shot up into the air like a pool noodle forced under water. We flew out.

I came up sputtering, the rapids first carrying me, then slowing around me. Immediately I grabbed for our runaway paddles.

I then turned to see my dad dizzily stand up only to fall right back down again.

"Are you okay?" I shouted, running toward him, slipping and falling in the water as I went.

But he just stood there, dazed. Only half of his pair of glasses remained on his face. His chin, nose, and forehead were bloodied and speckled with tree bark. His shirt was shredded like it had been attacked by a feral cheese grater.

"Dad!" I bellowed, tossing the paddles into our now unmanned canoe.

Still stunned, my dad began inspecting his arms and legs, assessing the damage, which was significant. The entire front of his body was covered in one continuous strawberry. He had twigs in his hair; dirt and bark were embedded in his skin.

My brother was now running up behind me. "Kristin!" he shouted.

"I'm okay! Look at Dad!"

We both trudged through the water toward our father.

Brian passed me. "Dad! Say something!"

My dad looked at us blankly. The remaining side of his glasses that stood on his face, with its lens entirely cracked, was now fogged and hazy. "I think that tree tore off my right nipple. One of you has to look," he said calmly and with complete sincerity.

And that's why I don't canoe anymore. I like my nipples right where they are.

Over the years, however, I've come, to think about the Universe like those lead canoes, shouting back to us from ahead. We hear its calls in the form of our gut instinct. Sometimes we listen. Sometimes we don't, and then under the oak tree we go.

I've always been a glass-half-full gal, so I believe that most of those shouts are meant to pull us toward our abundance and not just warn us from our sorrows. The Universe is just too good a stern woman or man to focus only on steering us *away*, when He or She can steer us *toward*.

I also believe that, even when the river goes wrong, it's most likely the right path for us. In the moment we might not be able to see it, but rejection protects us from the outcomes that are not meant for us. Failure steels us for the road ahead.

Maybe that's just the optimist in me speaking, but that's how I see the world.

I once had a client tell me that I was like one of those blow-up clowns with the weighted stones in the bottom. No matter how hard or how many times a kid punches that clown in the face, it pops right back up again. Smack, smack, and boing. Each time.

You know what? It's a fair assessment. Even I'll be the first to admit that I have an almost violent level of optimism.

To be honest, weapons of mass destruction feel like such small dick energy to me, especially when we have optimism at our disposal. Optimism is the real power move. It can shift everything on its axis.

Our brains, default to the "sky is falling mode." It takes a lot of hard work to tune them to the "everything is as it should be station," instead. I'm not talking by employing denial or toxic positivity, here. *Those* are rooted in ego. Optimism is anchored in energy.

True optimism, in fact, is a much deeper practice than positivity. It's a framework that says, "I see the dark cloud, but I am not going to focus on it. Conversely, I see the silver lining, but I'm not going to obsess over that either. I'm going to frame the *full* picture, instead. That includes what I bring to the situation, what I can control, and what I can't. That framework tells me everything I need to know. It shows me that things might fall apart, but my powerful energy could also make them come together. Either way, no matter what happens *inside* the picture, the frame will remain strong. *It* will maintain its structure."

Optimism is that frame.

In practical terms, real optimism isn't starved for positivity. It hungers expansion. To expand we need both success *and* setbacks, both bring about our abundance. In practice, optimism looks and feels like resiliency.

If I didn't have optimism as my anchor and resiliency as my sail, my ship would have sunk a long time ago because the world doesn't *just* work out. *We* work out the world. To do that, we need a massive energy reserve.

I believe optimism and resiliency are our two greatest generators for that energy. Think of them like the Hoover Dam. Together, they're the barrier that helps us process, channel, harness, and hold back the world around us. All these life-events coming down the river, and it's up to us to filter through them in a controlled way. If we remove the damn, we lose that chance and could end up drowning in all of it.

But, with our dam in place, we get to look at what is coming downstream and frame it, so we can then use it to generate direction, momentum, and more energy in our lives.

Over the course of my career, my optimism has been tested. I'm not talking sometimes. I'm talking all the time.

Every set I walk onto, nearly half the people don't want me there. Actually, let's call a spade, a spade, most times none of them want me there. When I'm in the role of talent manager, they want me to move out of the way so that they can get to my talent. Easier to manipulate the talent if I'm not there whispering in their ear. When I'm in the role of EP (executive producer), they'd like me to be quiet because, more often than not, they don't believe I earned the right to that title.

Here's a list of jabs other EPs or heads of development have said to me on set:

"I guess every manager thinks they're an EP now, huh?"

"So, what are they just giving the titles out these days to anyone?"

"The other EPs and producers are pretty upset because they earned their titles."

"That meeting was for actual producers, not just named ones. So...."

"A negotiation got you your title. My resume got me mine."

Each day a different battle of the wills. Constant undermining. Potshots. Insults. In the end, though, I almost always make my way out of their burn books and onto their group chat lists. Not because I'm good at my job — which of course I am — but because I am as good at my *job* as I am my *shadow* job.

A shadow job is all the work we do behind the scenes of *each* relationship we are in to navigate the power balance or imbalance of that relationship. It's maneuvering the behaviors, egos, and personalities of the people in our lives in the hopes of maintaining a sense of autonomy, authority, or mutual expansion within the relationship.

In her *Real Housewives of Beverly Hills* season five opener, LVP, gave us all a tag line for what happens when we're good at our shadow jobs. She said, "Throw me to the wolves, Darling, and I'll return leading the pack." It's a line I like to say to myself as I step onto every new set or project.

Every relationship, partnership, or pairing requires a certain amount of shadow work. I'm talking even with our own damn mothers. Heck, even with our own damn selves.

Of all the energy sucks of our shadow jobs, dealing with people who have insecurity about our personal power has to be the most tiresome. In fact, the more personal power we possess, the greater *their* insecurity grows. How dare we be strong? Time and time again that insecurity compels them to try and exert their emotional control over us. It's because *they* feel emotionally out of control around us.

We aren't doing this to them, of course. They are doing *this* to themselves. The rabbit out of their hat is to try and blame us for this, but like every other magic trick, that's just the illusion they are selling *to* themselves.

It's frustrating when it is happening. It's exhausting. It's draining. It's toxic. But it is also a giant billboard for this truth: They are afraid that we might outgrow them — or maybe we already have.

The simple fact is, most often when we expand and others don't, we either hang back to accommodate them or move forward without them. Watching them resist this is hard, but we can't let anyone else be the deciding factor for which path we choose.

We have to get in our boat and listen for the Universe shouting back to us from two canoes ahead, relying on our two best paddles of optimism and resiliency. They are what will get us through when the river runs wild, making sure we come out the other side of the oak tree, nipples and all.

NINE

The Witching Hour

"I don't know what you want me to say. This is the first time I've ever pooped my pants in public. So, I don't know the protocol."

I stared at my mother as we stood on a small sidewalk in downtown Newport, Rhode Island.

Her look of condemnation faded and gave way to a full hysterical laugh.

"Go ahead. Laugh. I'm going to the car." I reached down and gathered my skirt around me like a diaper and shuffle-walked toward the SUV.

About ten years prior, I had visited Newport for the first time while in Rhode Island for a friend's wedding. As is the case for every trip I take, I had researched pawn shops and antiques stores in the area and then booked an extra day of my trip to zig zag across Newport in search of estate jewelry and vintage finds.

First stop was a drive over the Pell Bridge right into the heart of Newport's quaint downtown with its immaculate neighborhoods and opulent Gilded Age mansions.

Within minutes of my arrival, this little town on Rhode Island's Narragansett Bay swept me off my feet.

I parked the rental car, bought a coffee, and walked to a small downtown park to enjoy my croissant. I sat sipping my latte and watching a group of women tie herbs together, cradle crystals before collecting them into pouches, and swap tiny bottles of oils to mix homemade tinctures.

"Can I ask," I called out, "what are you all up to?"

"It's a powerful eclipse tonight," one said, "and we're preparing for our moon ritual."

Another added, "It's an especially magical day for your sacral goddess." Her eyes glistened with excitement at the thought.

Any town where witches can meet at dawn and ride at the stroke of midnight is my kind of place. It took everything in me not to ask to join their coven.

Caffeinated, I strolled the downtown main street, visiting all the shops with their endless inventories of art, pottery, painted silk scarves, and handmade jewelry. Every woman I passed looked like my college art history professor,

draped in eight layers of linen and an armful of bangles —
or me in ten years, as it would turn out.

"Are you an artist?" a shop owner asked as I stood in his
store admiring his handmade "junk pots." There was a
calligraphy sign hanging above the pots, telling the story
of how each was constructed out of rolled clay before
being fancifully painted with vegetable-dyed inks.

"No," I said, smiling.

"Huh, I'm normally a good guesser as to what people do."
He sounded wounded at reading me wrong.

"Do you work in fashion?" the woman in the boutique two
doors down asked as I perused her racks of linen dresses
and gauzy tops.

"No."

"A designer of some sort, then?" she pressed.

I waffled. "Not really," I finally offered.

"Hm," she intoned, handing me the sterling silver
necklace I had asked about in one of the cases.

In each store, it seemed the clerk, sales associate, artist,
or owner wanted to guess about me, this girl in a drapey
silk dress, high crown rancher hat, and cowgirl boots.

I continued making my way down the block until I found myself standing in a general store of sorts. It felt more artist's studio than today's more common take on a general store. The tables of the shop were laden with handmade potions, woven baskets, and jewelry. The shelves were lined with art, ceramics, and locally made hats. The fixtures were as beautiful as the store's contents, each constructed of rough-hewn wood and iron.

"My husband made me each of those fixtures in his woodshed in the back of our house," the shop owner shared as she watched me admire a hat on a top shelf. "Wanna try it on?" she asked.

I turned toward her. She was eyeing me from under a fringe of silver bangs.

I nodded yes.

"I have to know what you do. I've been trying to read your energy since you walked in," she shared as she climbed up on a ladder to retrieve the hat for me. Her armful of bangles clinked together with every move she made.

She handed the hat down to me from the top rung of her ladder.

I placed it on my head and turned to look at her. "It's funny, in each store I've gone into, the owner or sales associate has taken a stab at decoding me."

"Really? What did they each say?"

"The first one thought I was an artist. The second a fashion designer or designer of some sort. Next door they asked if I was a jewelry designer."

"And you aren't *any* of those things?" she asked, giving me a love-the-hat nod as I looked at my reflection in the mirror.

"Not really," I said, handing the hat over to her. "I'm for sure taking the hat." *As a PS, I always buy the hat. I'm like a homing pigeon for millinery.*

The shop owner looked at me, her red readers perched low on her nose, her aubergine silk scarf swirled around her neck. "I don't buy it for a second. I feel like in some way you're all those things. I can feel that you're very powerful. Do you know that about yourself?" Before I could answer, she issued a diagnosis. "Oh wait, that's the problem. You *don't* know that about yourself, do you?"

I felt bowled over by this stranger's psychological reading of me.

"Tell me," she said, gesturing to a stool at the cash rep, "tell me all about you. I want *you* to hear it for yourself, *from* yourself."

She walked around the glass merchandise case and perched on a stool on the other side where she patiently sipped her tea and politely waited for me to begin. She was like a spiritual mobster. I felt compelled to share with her. So, I sat down, slung the strap of my purse around my knees so it wouldn't rest on the floor, and began.

We talked for nearly two hours. Customers came in, shopped, eavesdropped, joined in the chat, and left, but we continued.

At a natural lull in the conversation, she said, "I love it when I'm right." *Witches can be so cocky, can't they?* "See? You *are* all those skills and art forms. You just haven't allowed yourself to own them. I'm not sure why that is, but whatever it is, *that's* going to be the life-long lesson for you to figure out. I just feel like you keep trying to earn something you already own."

The violence, I thought. *Just shoot me already.*

I had never been so called into the circle of myself before in my life. I was always the one doing the reading, the assessing, the intuitive diagnosis of the people around me. Somehow, though, I had forgotten to turn that cauldron on myself.

And, of course, like all the other witches of Newport, this one was a thousand percent correct. Owning my success, my skills, the IP of me has been a lifelong struggle. Not that this struggle has stopped me from having a tremendous output of creativity. It hasn't. I am an idea factory. And, along the way so many I've encountered in my life have been more than eager to claim that creativity as their own. For some reason, though, I have not afforded myself that same ownership.

I have stood in rooms clapping and cheering for each person on the team as they were called out in recognition of their contribution. My name was not said. Everyone, including me, heard that silence.

I have sat in the wings and watched as each team member was brought onto the stage for the project group photo, and I felt my heart break when I was excluded.

I have sat on calls as someone on the other end bitterly questioned my role with, "Who does she *even* think she is to ask for this?" when I was the one who developed the project.

These exclusions are painful. The message, again and again, is something akin to a line I said all the time to my classroom of kids when I was preschool teacher, "You get what you get, and you don't throw a fit."

That line has merit for snack time, but it is no longer relevant to us as we own our capabilities, strengths, and success in the workplace or in the dynamic of our relationships.

What we <u>do not</u> claim for ourselves, others will take for their own use, and make no mistake, they'll keep coming back to take more.

But, when we own the mountain, we no longer need to question our right to climb it.

This land of myself has been parceled up again and again by those eager to stake their claim to it, but several years ago I decided no more. Each day and each boundary since sent up the flare declaring that a revolution has come.

Mine.

"I'm gonna give you a coin," the shop owner said, carefully placing my hat in a hatbox. "It's for the Pell bridge. It used to take toll tokens to come across it. Growing up we gave them to guests, so they'd come back. Of course, now the tokens are all gone, replaced by credit cards and transponders, but my family kept a few as keepsakes. We cherish them. I even have one framed in a shadow box on my gallery wall." She pointed behind the register where one framed gold coin floated on its backdrop of black linen.

"I want you to have one. I want you to know that there are people here who *really* hope you'll come back."

She smiled as she placed the token in my hand, closing my fingers around it and then clasping her hands around mine. "Now you don't have an excuse *not* to return," she winked.

After the sale of my first talk show, which was nearly eight years after that first trip to Newport, I moved to New

York. I wanted to be there for the 70+ hour work weeks I knew it would require to through the launch.

Most new talk shows fail. In fact, there is a graveyard filled with them. Sorry Jeff Probst and Tempestt Bledsoe. Talk shows are so complex; each is its own entertainment start-up that is required to get off the ground and score a rating immediately or it's almost always deemed a failure.

This launch was no different. The lead up to premiere day was frenzied with work and high emotions. I was exhausted, mentally and physically.

On one of our only breaks, I decided a weekend road trip was in order.

I told my mom and aunt about all the possibilities up the coast. I hadn't even finished asking if they wanted to go when each blurted out, "Yes! We're in!" on our three-way call.

One week and one flight later both arrived in New York City.

We loaded our luggage and Merna into the rental car and hit the road, driving through Connecticut, Rhode Island, and on into Maine. We stayed in quaint Airbnb's along the way and sipped fresh lemonades and iced lattes as we drove, stopping in every small town we came across.

In Connecticut we went to Mystic Pizza for pizza, of course. If you haven't seen the film by the now, then all I can say to you is, "How dare you?" It's only one of the best rom coms of all time *and* the first time any of us ever *really* met our beloved Queen Julia Roberts on screen.

Along the way, we decided to challenge ourselves with a taste test, stopping to critique every lobster roll we encountered. It was a strange mission, really, because I don't actually like seafood. I know, it's crazy. I have routinely tried to talk myself into believing otherwise. *You just have to find the right recipe,* I reason with myself. Twice now, I have attempted What's Gaby Cooking and Geri Hirsch's respective salmon recipes. My brain says yes. My tastebuds say no.

On this trip, however, I was determined to get my inner New Englander on.

As we came across the Pell Bridge into Newport, we collectively gasped. There's no sign at the city limits telling you to do so, but I think it's mandatory. Newport is just that pretty.

We then drove the streets admiring the beauty, saying ridiculous things like, "I'm not sure what they're thinking with those pillars," and "Who came up with that layout?" — as if we wouldn't take any one of the gilded mansions Newport has to offer, in a heartbeat.

We checked into our adorable Airbnb, swooned over its view, and headed out to grab sandwiches.

"We should get them to go so we can go the beach."

"Absolutely," my mom and aunt agreed.

I am a mountain girl, but of all the air I have ever breathed, salt air is by far the most intoxicating. Can we all agree on this?

With our sandwiches in hand, we drove until we found a small patch of beach just off the road. I pulled in and opened the windows and the sunroof. I then laid our sandwiches across the dash, placing our deli salads on the center console. Our car picnic was set.

We sat quietly eating and watching the swimmers and sunbathers, murmuring to one another about how delicious the sandwiches were, smiling like someone had piped nitrous gas into the car. It was exactly as you picture it. Vacation bliss.

"Is it just me or is this bread a spiritual experience?" I asked.

"I know," my mom declared, chewing a bite of her tuna fish on homemade sourdough.

It was so idyllic that none of us saw the trouble that was lurking ahead for us as we dove into our communal lobster roll.

"The sandwiches were a ten, but the lobster roll...no...too much mayo," my mom said as she used a paper towel to capture the globs of mayonnaise that had oozed down the back of her hand when she took a bite.

"A hundred percent," my aunt said.

"Hey," I said interrupting, "I think we should go in the water. Our towels and suits are in the back." I smiled at them both expectantly.

My aunt Phyllis looked at me like I was crazy. "You two go. I'll stay in the car with Merna."

I caught my mother's eye in the rearview mirror, "You in?"

She stared out at the water. "I mean, we *are* right here," she reasoned.

I nodded excitedly to encourage a full yes.

We were out of the car and changing at the back hatch in no time, doing the old towel wrapped around the waist trick so you can trade your pants for a bathing suit bottom in broad daylight at a public beach.

Gingerly, we made our way across the rocks onto the sand and from there wasted no time wading into the water. We smiled at the kids splashing in the shallow waves and nodded our heads at the women languidly floating on their rafts.

"Is this bay freshwater or is it a mix of saltwater from the open sea out there?" I pointed toward the horizon.

"I don't know, maybe it's.... Ouch!" my mom shouted suddenly.

I spun to look at her. I'm not necessarily afraid of open water. One of my best life experiences *was* swimming in the deep ocean with wild and free dolphins. But an exclamation of ouch when you can't see to the bottom will always spark terror in me. I have seen *Jaws,* after all.

"What's wrong?" I asked, peering worriedly into the water around me.

"I felt a pinch."

"A pinch?"

"I don't know, a bite." Reading my alarm, she collected herself and rephrased, "It must have been a rock or something."

On full alert, we stood watching the other beachgoers until we heard my aunt shouting for us. We turned back toward shore to find her waving her camera out the car window, gesturing for us to pose. We did so, laughing and smiling.

"We good?" I asked.

My mom nodded.

"No murderous seaweed getting you?"

"Very funny," she said as we tenuously lowered ourselves back down into the water.

The waves lulled us, and we began to float further out.

"Look at that boat," I pointed toward the horizon.

"Gorgeous," my mom agreed. "Can you imagine," she began, but stopped suddenly, kicking her legs toward the bottom as she let out a grunt. "Uhhhh!"

I pushed away from her in the water. "Stop it. It's not funny."

She reached out and grabbed my arm, pulling me toward her through the waves. "Do I have a bite?" she asked, turning her neck to the side so I could look at her collar bone.

"I don't think so."

"Are you sure? LOOK."

"I'm looking at you. I don't see anything."

My mom just stared at me.

"Shantelle!" I shouted, using the nickname I've called my mother for more than a decade now.

"Something's biting me," she said dramatically. "I feel it!"

"There's nothing here," I said looking at the water around us. The sun now overhead allowed me to see all the way to my feet. "I don't see what could be biting you."

She looked around, panicked. "I don't know. I think something's in my bathing suit." She stood and yanked at her bathing, pulling it away from her body, the suction of the fabric making a "thwack" sound when it finally pulled away from her skin.

"What are you doing, Shantelle?" I began to laugh at her.

She flung herself toward me. "Something's in my suit. You have to look." She stared at me pointedly. Her face was filled with terror. "NOW!" she demanded.

"Okay," I calmed.

Hesitantly, I took a step forward, cautiously peering down the front of her suit.

"What's there?" she panicked. I could hear the fear in her voice.

"Your boobs," I said. I was now on the razor's edge between full blown hysterical laughter and terror. Involuntarily, I began to giggle harder.

"Stop it," she demanded. "Something's there."

"Shantelle. I don't see anything,"

"Ahhhhh!" she shrieked.

I jumped back and fell into the water.

She plunged forward, clutching at me again.

"It's still biting me! You have to get it!"

"Get what? Nothing's there. Have you gone mad?" I asked her.

"Look again," she demanded.

Once again, I peered down the front of my mother's bathing suit. "What am I *even* looking for?"

"I don't know!" she said. And, then with a growing alarm, she added, "A creature?"

"A creature?" I asked, echoing her.

She shrugged her shoulders and let out a gurgled whimper.

"Shantelle, there is nothing in the front of your suit. I promise."

I then watched my bewildered mother stare down the front of her own swimsuit before proceeding to reach her entire arm up to her elbow down in and grope around her waistline.

"Are you literally crazy right now, Shantelle? People are staring at us." I looked around, smiling weakly at a trio of girls who were openly gaping at the scene we were making.

My aunt would tell us later that she was extremely worried for us, watching the entire scene unfold but unable to understand what was going on. *"When you screamed, I screamed. I don't know why. You two were acting like you were being attacked, but everyone else was just fine. I didn't know what to do. Call 911 to help you or freak out and get arrested with you."*

Still groping herself, my mother remained unpersuaded, "And nothing's biting you?" she accused, her eyes searching mine.

"Nothing," I assured her.

Again, we stood, staring at one another, waves from a passing boat jostling us in the water. A few moments of calm passed between us before my mother looked around and realized that a hundred other people were in full summer mode. Laughing. Playing. Splashing.

Defeated, she sat back down in the water. We began to drift once again in the waves.

"I can't wait for tomorrow. I told you I brought my token, right?"

She nodded with excitement. We were floating side by side now, staring at the horizon, our feet sticking up and out of the water as we used our hands to stay afloat.

"I hope that shop owner is still there. How cool would it be to see her after all these years, right?" My face shone bright with the daydream of the idea.

"Do you think she'd remember you?" Shantelle asked.

I went to speak when I suddenly felt a searing pain, "OUCH!" I shouted.

Without hesitation my mother turned and dove toward shore. "Fuck this beach," she shouted behind her, swiftly kicking her legs to get away from me.

The water was up to our necks at this point.

"GAAAAHHHHH!" I cried out.

"Fucking stay away from me!" she instructed as she lunged forward toward the beach.

I reached after her, grabbing for her. When I made contact with her arm, she shook me off like a kid who slips out of his windbreaker to allude being hauled out of the Chuck E. Cheese.

"Shantelle!" I begged.

"You're on your fucking own," she said, as she swam away from me.

"Mooommm!" I screamed.

"I can't help you!" she shouted back. "No one can help you!"

When we got to where we could both stand, it was my turn to pull my swimsuit away from my body. I stared inside the lowcut V of the front. My mom looked on in horror. Initially, she stood back from me, about four feet away, but slowly she stepped forward until she, too, was peering down into my swimsuit.

Breathless with fear, we searched my front. Nothing was there.

"Ahhhhh!" I flinched. We both jumped.

I grabbed her arm as I held my suit out, wrenching her back toward me. "What's in there?" I begged.

"Nothing," she cried. "I don't see anything."

"You're lying!"

We were both nearly hysterical at this point.

I steadied myself before reaching down the front and rooting around under my breast where I had felt the pain. When my finger brushed something, I pinched it between my two fingers and pulled my hand out. Together my mother and I leaned in. I held my hand up above us toward the sunlight. There on my finger sat a tiny, translucent crab. We peered up at it, its tiny, nearly invisible claws opening and closing in the air. The only non-translucent element were its coal black eyes, both of which sat atop two tiny, creepy antennae, staring back at us.

In unison, with our faces no less than four inches apart, we screamed bloody murder. I flung the crab from my finger. My aunt would tell us later that she, too, screamed again in the car, even though she still had no idea what was happening to us.

Simultaneously, my mom and I looked from my finger back down into the blue saltwater. Bravely, my mother cupped her hands together, dipped them below the surface, and raised them back up. Holding our breath, we watched the water pour up and over the sides of her hands until a horror show emerged.

There in her palms sat at least forty crabs, their clear pinchers chomping at the air. A thousand beady eyes staring up at us. With the water gone, a frenzy set in. The crabs began a mad dash, first crawling up her wrists and then racing wildly up onto her arms.

With a look of sheer panic, we screamed into one another's face. My aunt, still completely in the dark as to what was happening, screamed in the car for a third time. The realization set in that it was *these* tiny crabs in the water that had been biting us the entire time, their teeny, transparent claws ripping us apart.

So naturally, we did the only imaginable thing to do. On a public beach in Rhode Island, with small children and families a mere ten feet from us, my mother and I, ripped down our respective bathing suit tops and began motor-boating our own breasts in the water, attempting to rid ourselves of these tiny invaders, screaming like banshees the entire time.

"Runnnn," I shrieked as I took off for the car, my swimsuit still fully falling off, my arms crossed over my bare breasts. I could hear my mother behind me in hot pursuit.

We didn't even towel off. We just dove into the car and drove away.

"There's one in my crotch," I screamed as I careened back toward our rental house. "It's biting me. I *literally* have crabs."

We were laughing so hard that we almost wrecked twice on the ride home.

After we showered and rechecked every square inch of ourselves for stowaways, we went to dinner to soothe our weary souls, a seafood restaurant of course. I remained committed to my New England tour and ordered the Branzino. My mother ordered a seafood stew that smelled like two seals were under our table, perhaps mating. It was so bad that we still talk about that stew. *"Remember when you ordered the mating seal goulash?"* I like to randomly ask my mother just so I can watch her turn green in the Target aisle.

Collectively grossed out, we decided to forgo our lobster roll for one evening. We were all tired and still, somewhat, shell-shocked from the crab attack earlier in the day.

"I can't wait to see that general store tomorrow," my mom said as we drove back to our Airbnb, all of us staring up at the inky midnight sky as we drove.

"Me too," I said. After the day we'd had, it felt good to have something to look forward to.

The next day, however, we found out that the general store was no longer there. In its place, a new shop stood on the downtown's main street. It was different from the general store I had visited but no less adorable. The new owner somehow magically still possessed some of the same energy as the previous owner, and we were captivated by her and her shop. My only guess it's a Rhode Island quirk. Warm hospitality is perhaps in their blood like the salt air. Every store is magical.

As with her predecessor, we stood talking to her with the ease of an old friend.

"What a great story," the owner said, as I regaled her with the tale of my previous visit. "I wish I knew who that was, but it's been quite a few years, and I'm not from around here originally. I just don't know who that would have been."

My mom and I nodded. "Well, we had to try. The story was too good to not come back, hoping the shop would still be here, you know?" my mom said.

"I'm so glad you did. Newport is pretty special, exactly for the reasons you're talking about. Do you still have the token?" the new proprietor asked, turning my direction.

She was beaming at me. I reached into my pocket to fish out the token when something *intruded* upon me. I realized, with great horror, that I was suddenly pooping my pants.

I could feel an anxious and angry look crash across my face. I aggressively turned and tore out of the store without saying a word, nearly pulling the door off the hinges as I went.

Once outside, I power walked about ten steps, before stopping to sweat and clutch a No Parking sign.

"Kristin Ann!" my mom shouted behind me, following me out of the shop and down the street. "Why didn't you answer her? What's wrong with you? Why are you running away?" she scolded.

"I just pooped my pants," I said distraught. Having taken three more steps, I was now hugging an emotional support parking meter.

Momentarily stunned, my mother went to speak but then closed her mouth in confusion. After a beat she tried again. "Wait, what?"

I didn't answer. I was too busy gathering my skirt up around me like a diaper.

"You pooped your pants? Like, right now?" she asked.

"Right now. As in, I think I am still actively pooping my pants. To be honest, I am unsure, okay?" I stared at her. "So you go in there and get Phyl because I have to go to the car and finish shitting myself in private, okay?"

"Do you need a bathroom?" my mom asked confused.

"Clearly, but that ship has sailed, Shantelle," I said as I waddled toward the car.

"What should I tell the woman?" my mom shouted after me.

"That I'm sorry I shit in her store!"

I could hear my mother and aunt wheezing with laughter all the way to the car.

After five hours of complete panic during which I felt totally fine yet, still, kept intermittingly pooping my pants, a tele-doctor informed me of the following:

"It sounds like you might have a slight seafood allergy, where your body isn't able to *really* process all the fish you've been having this week. As a result, it's stopped breaking it down properly, and at this point you're just leaking out the fish oil. My best guess is that you could be, intermittently, leaking for a week, maybe longer."

Guess what? He was right. I shit myself in a Starbucks, a sandwich shop, and in a packed elevator. To this day, nothing incites terror in me, like a fish fry.

My yelp review on Branzino will forever remain, "The fish is wonderful. The anal leakage is less so."

But here's the point: I don't regret throwing myself after a challenge or trying something new. In fact, I think the number one ingredient we need more of in our lives is a sense of discovery. We have become passive in how we receive information, watching it on our tiny screens. As a result, we are living in a curiosity famine, and our sense of discovery is quickly diminishing.

We are currently mistaking manifesting and goal setting as the preferred actions while dismissing the roles discovery and curiosity play in our lives, our relationships, and in ourselves.

The person I am most surprised to have met in my life is me. And I meet her again and again. Each time I do, she is different. I am different. That is because I am actively seeking self-discovery on my path.

Don't get me wrong, I manifest like a mother! Full stop. But I also make room for something else, daydreaming. The art of imagining our lives is as essential as manifesting them. When we manifest, our mind says, "This is the goal." Our energy then aligns to pull that goal towards us.

But what happens when what we are manifesting is a safe narrative of ourselves, or the version of ourselves that our mind has already decided that we worked too hard *just* to abandon it now? That path ignores the daydream of mapping a very different path with its more-wild possibilities.

Discovery is about unearthing what is unexpected in ourselves. Manifesting is mining for what is anticipated. Both energies are needed. I encourage, though, that we pursue them in the correct order. Otherwise, discovery dies on the vine of our lives.

And it's not about *just* trying something new. It is about *specifically* trying what we are afraid we won't be good at or be capable of doing. That's the only way we can expand the understanding of ourselves. Trying what scares us is so often the only bridge that leads to the road that is fully meant for us.

So I say, do what we think we can't – do what others tell us we can't — that's how we meet the moments *and* the people that will change us, like the witches of Newport changed me. And, yes, that means sometimes we will indeed shit the bed. But, I believe we have to do it anyway and pack an extra pair of pants just in case.

TEN

Pop the Trunk

"What do you mean you gave the trunk away?"

My oma stared at me from the stove where she stood using tongs to pile bacon onto a Corelle plate. I reached out for the dish, but she took it back, apparently now holding it hostage as she awaited my answer.

"Well, I had a friend who needed a TV stand, and I asked him if he'd like to use it."

I gently took the plate, grabbed the pot of coffee from the coffeemaker, and walked to the breakfast table with both.

"Why? How?"

"Well, my loft is smaller, and the trunk is a really big piece. I realized I just don't have a spot for it."

She flipped two eggs.

"We found that trunk in the flood, floating in four feet of water in our neighbor's basement. Opa carried it home in the pouring rain. It took weeks to dry out, and you *just* give it away?"

I was circling the table, filling each coffee cup.

"I didn't *just* give it away. I used that trunk for more than a decade and I loved it," I said, compassionately.

Although, between you and me, that wasn't exactly the truth. I had never actually liked the trunk, but now was not the time.

I finished filling the last cup and sat down at the table. I could feel her eyeing me. We began to pass the plate of bacon around. She clicked off the burner, carried the skillet of eggs over to the table, and stood over me. I held out my plate so that she could dish one egg out to me. She, of course, ignored this altogether and proceeded to slide one fried egg onto each place setting except mine.

"I don't understand. Why didn't you give _us_ the trunk?" she asked, putting the skillet down just out of my reach.

Oh the pettiness of the family breakfast.

"I didn't even know you would want it. Honestly."

"Of course I would want it back. It's our trunk," she said defensively.

"Well, it's actually my trunk," I carefully offered.

My father aggressively cleared his throat to get my attention. I looked at him across the table. He raised his eyebrows as the universal communication of "Please drop this. You are home for only four days. Let's not ruin it, shall we?"

I turned back to my grandmother and paused. "I'm sorry you're upset. It didn't dawn on me that you would want it back."

"That trunk came over on the Mayflower, you know?"

I looked at her. Reading her. She was, of course, dead serious.

"Uhhhhh, I'm not sure about that. The hinges looked too new."

She stared at me, frowned deeply, and shrugged, "Well, we guess you would know. It's your trunk, right?" She nodded at my Opa. Everything was always a "we," in their household when you were on the spot.

I looked at my dad. He shook his head no, so imperceptivity that I wasn't even sure he had done it. I took another breath.

"Listen, I've loved that trunk for years. You both know that." I smiled at my grandfather. "I'm grateful you gave it to me. It's gone through six apartments with me, but, unfortunately, I'm moving and just don't have a spot for it anymore."

She stared at me blankly, like how a mob boss listens to a lieutenant whom he knows is stealing from him — a put-on air of support, if you will.

"It's gone to a really great home. And…"

She opened her mouth to interrupt, but I gently put my hand over hers to quiet her. "And, when my friend is done with it, I'll get it back, alright?"

She eyed me suspiciously. "Well, what can we do? What's done is done," she finally said.

Of course, she and I both knew it wasn't done. The truth was that it would not be *done*, until I got the trunk back.

The reality of my oma was this: She was allowed to return any gift we gave her, and in fact, *did* return nearly every gift we gave her. It was the food chain of gift giving in our family. We gave her gifts. She took them back.

The gifts she gave us, however, were never allowed to be returned. We were to love and adore each one of them, unwaveringly so, and in perpetuity. I'm talking even if the pants didn't fit, you just moved on, squeezed into them, and wore them at the next family dinner anyway.

The trunk in question was given to me as a senior in high school. It was more of "Do you think you might have a spot for this?" conversation in which I said, "Sure." It wasn't given with great fanfare or even for a birthday. It was a "Hey we rescued this and fixed it up. Maybe you can use it," sort of thing. Giving it away, after fifteen years of use, didn't feel like I was emotionally abandoning an heirloom. Of course, my oma clearly felt otherwise.

The next day, I received the first of many phone calls, "I'm so sick. Up all night. Throwing up," she said hoarsely into the receiver of her landline.

"Oh gosh. Was it the eggs?" I feigned ignorance.

"What? No. I was up because I'm *worried* about that trunk. What if your friend ruins it? I think you best call him. Tell him we need it back. Opa's very upset."

"Where are you going to put it?"

"We called the neighbor. They said they'd take it."

"So, just to be clear, you want me to get the trunk back from *my* friend, who's using it, drive it all eight hours back to Ohio, so that *you* can give it *away* to a neighbor. How is that different than me offering it to *my* friend?"

"Well, it's *our* trunk."

"Again, it's actually *my* trunk. You gave it to me 15 years ago."

I heard a dramatic sigh on the other end. "Well, if you aren't upset about it, then how can we be, right?"

A moment of silence passed. She sighed again. "You know what? I'll just tell the neighbors they can't have it now. I hope they'll understand."

I bit my tongue. "Okay," I whispered quietly, "I'll talk to my friend when I get back to Chicago."

"Only if you want to. Like you said, it's your trunk."

I clutched the phone's receiver so hard that I hurt my own hand.

My mom and I left the next morning for my return to Chicago. My moving day was two days away. I was officially a homeowner. Of course, an hour into our drive, I got word that I was needed in New York. A photo shoot I had planned for the following week was moving up. My mom and I quickly devised a plan for her to oversee my move.

As we drove, my phone rang off the hook with producers calling with details for the shoot and my oma calling with worries about the trunk. She called twice in Indiana, alone.

"Maybe I call your friend. Opa can't sleep. What if he throws the trunk out? We need to make sure he knows it's our trunk."

"He's not going to throw it out. I promise you. I already told you I would talk to him about getting it back."

My mom shook her head in the passenger seat.

"What if he already sold it? He could do that, you know?" my oma pressed.

"He's not going to sell it," I confirmed.

"I don't know. I can't eat without knowing for sure. You have to be sure," she said with true grief.

When I hung up, my mom asked, half laughing, half outraged, "Why did you *even* tell her about the trunk?"

"Because I'm an idiot."

"Clearly," my mom agreed, "first rule of Oma is tell her nothing."

"I know!" I howled. "I fucked up."

"What are you gonna do?"

"Hope she forgets about it," I said.

My mom and I then howled with laughter at that thought, because we both knew the likelihood of that happening was nil to zero.

After an eight-hour drive, we arrived back in Chicago at 8 p.m. that night. And, by 5 a.m. the next morning, I was rushing out the door to get to O'Hare airport while my mother was already up and furiously bubble-wrapping the last of the kitchen.

Within two days, I had covered off on my cover shoot, and my mother had orchestrated my entire move without me.

I have to admit it was a little strange not to be there for my move but also deliciously wonderful to have someone else deal with it. If you're ever given the chance, I highly recommend. Ten out of ten. Except for the pro tip to hide your vibrator better than I did. To my mother who is undoubtedly reading this book, I would like to apologize once again for the scare.

When I finally walked through the door two days later, I found my mother in the kitchen organizing my cupboards.

"I started a *sell* and *donate* pile. I figured, I'm not puttin' things away that you aren't plannin' to keep," my mom shouted at me as I hauled my luggage up the spiral staircase to my new bedroom.

"Totally!" I shouted down over the railing.
The next three days were a continuous loop of opening, emptying, and then hauling boxes to the recycling center, stopping only to buy more coffee or take-out along the way.

As we worked, the donation and sell piles grew quickly.

"Charity's great and all, you know? But you have that *whole* minivan downstairs to fill. You might as well load it up and see what we can sell this summer. I'm for sure doing a garage sale, and whatever doesn't go I can donate on the other end," my mom explained as she piled canned goods into the pantry.

It's astonishing the number of tchotchkes one person can amass. Somewhere along the line people had started giving me cat things. I'm not exactly sure why, but I think it had to do with the fact that I had a cat named Jersey.

Personally, I'm more of a ceramics nut with an overall postmodern meets 70s Italian aesthetic. But, like a nickname you can't shake, so is the arc of the perceived collection. Once others assign it to you, it's hard to break them of the habit. Take my aunt and uncle for example. They're pig farmers. For years we bought them pig things. A pig doorstop. A pig wall sign. A pig pillow. Finally my aunt sat us down and said, "No more pigs. Got it?"

One by one my mother and I placed all the cat cast-offs onto the sell tarp — along with a zillion other trinkets I had no recollection of buying.

First came a porcelain Siamese cat lamp. It was hollow and sat on a tiny pedestal. Inside was a small nightlight bulb. When turned on, the seemingly cute cat morphed into a total horror show. Its sunken eyes deepened, and the beige of its glaze cast a sickly color across the room.

Next came a cat shaped tea kettle. Its stopper was a tiny plastic mouse. When it whistled, it made a bizarre mewing sound that signaled to its owner time to make tea or finish murdering this half-dead cat that you left on your stove.

Then came the pièce de résistance, a 3-foot-tall cat Santa with a giant bag of presents slung over his shoulder. His face was painted in a demonic grin. He looked evil, like he might burn the house down as you slept. After I had opened him on Christmas day, I placed him under the tree. My cat viciously attacked him and then tried to pee on him, *twice.*

By the time my mom was ready to drive back to Ohio, the minivan was stacked full to the roof, but after she left, I forgot entirely about the garage sale. She never mentioned it on any of our near-daily calls until randomly one Sunday summer evening she rang.

"Hey?" she sang into the phone.

"Where have you guys been all weekend? I tried calling twice on Saturday," I replied.
"We had our garage sale," she gushed.

"What? When? You didn't mention you were having it this week."

"I know. I woke up on Thursday and said, it's now or never. I forced your father and aunt to help me. And guess what?"

"What?"

I could feel her excitement spilling over the phone lines.

"You sold three thousand dollars worth of stuff this weekend!"

"Whaaaat? Hoooow?"

"Well, all your stuff went and Oma and Opa had a whole heap of junk, including a washer and dryer and a bunch of tools. It all sold, and they said whatever money they made could go to you, to put toward your mortgage."

"What?!" I screamed.

"I know!" she shouted back.

Here's the thing about my grandparents, they could be very generous. For many years they volunteered their time at nursing homes. My grandfather would play his button box, and my oma would get the residents up and dancing. Not only that, they also routinely made nice gestures like gifting us money at Christmas, helping with college, and paying for books. They even bought me my first car.

But, and this is a big but, their generosity came with strings and stipulations.

"This car is so you can go to work," my oma explained as I slid behind the driver seat of the used Reliant K-Car they had purchased for me on my 16th birthday. They just randomly called me over, and there she was parked in their driveway, Lyn — the nickname I gave to her.

My oma leaned into the car window and said, "No friends in the car and only to and from work."

It took me days to talk them off that ledge. Not of the job. I've had a job since I was 14, but the 'no friends' rule.

Monetary gifts were common, but so was the manipulation that surrounded them. Money, and the control it exerts, is a real factor in many relationships. All gifts, really, can come with impositions if the giver deems it so. Generosity, just like everything, *can* be weaponized.

Sort of like how narcissists give lavish gifts that are ultimately meant to make them look good. The gift is a means to validate the narcissist's generosity and goodness as well as provide him or her a way to manipulate the power structure in the relationship. A favorite trick of narcissists is to then act like it's about you, but it's always about them and how they can get the esteem of others for having given the gift or how they can lord it over you for their future benefit.

If you're wondering right now if that fits anyone in your current life, consider this: Has that person ever said to your friends, "Did you see the gift I gave her?" or declared to you, "That gift was a lot, but I wanted *you* to have it. Remember that."

Classic narcissists.

My oma wasn't a narcissist. She was just controlling and opiniated. But I have dealt with one —or twelve — individuals in my life who were *for sure* clinical examples of narcissists. I will be unfolding the number *those* individuals did on me for years.

As for the garage sale and my grandparents donating their earnings to me, I wasn't sure how that would come back around, but I knew it would. My oma had expressed to me that she was disappointed I had purchased my condo. "I don't get why a woman would be out there doing things that ought to be done by a man."

But that was a problem for another day. Today, I was three thousand dollars richer, and nothing was going to get in the way of that fact. Not even my Oma.

Honestly, garage sales are the Midwestern answer for "How'd you pay for that?" As a kid growing up in Ohio, I learned never to underestimate the earning power of a well-planned, well-priced garage sale. It'll fund a trip to Italy if you time it right.

That Christmas I drove home for the holidays from Chicago, just as I always had, and we set out to enjoy our family's traditions, one being to have Christmas Eve at my oma and opa's house. As always, we ate dinner, did the dishes, put on coffee, and then sat down to open presents.

I should tell you, Christmas has always been big in our household. Beyond the decorating, my mom has always been a true innovator at Christmas time. It's a tradition that began when we were kids and continues until this very day.

She started her yuletide mastery with her present-hiding skills by brazenly hiding all of our presents within inches of my brother and me. We, of course, had no idea, despite how hard we looked for them. And, trust me, we looked.

"I'm going to the store," she'd holler, searching her purse for her keys.

We'd watch out the window until we saw her silver Cavalier disappear down the alley. Then, we'd rip the house apart looking for our presents. We were stealthy. One of us would be lookout as the other crawled to the back of the closet. We weren't sloppy either. We conducted our search room by room and floor by floor. We were methodical, using our mother's own words against her, "If you do it right the first time, you won't waste time retracing your steps."

Stop number one was always our parent's bedroom. Logic was that if our parents were buying us presents, they were — for sure — hiding them in their room. Each year we searched. Each year we came up emptyhanded.

From there, we'd move on to the attic, the basement, and even our own bedrooms. We never found anything, not even a single stocking stuffer.

Little did we know that the entire time my mother was hiding our presents in our family room. The two large barrel tables that stood at opposite ends of our sofa — draped in their matching blue, ruffled tablecloths — were hollow. For seven years we searched, having no idea.

Then, when I was eight, my brother told me he had figured it out. Yet, he refused to tell me what he had learned. Of all the betrayals — like getting shotgun on every car ride because he was 6feet tall in the 6th grade — this was the deepest cut from my brother.

"You'll never figure it out," he taunted as he played a video game on his Commodore 64.

   "Tell me," I begged.

"You wish," he teased.

And I did wish. But he never broke. When we moved four years later — and I still hadn't solved the mystery of the present hiding spot — my mom took pity on me. She *finally* told me where she had hidden our presents all those years before. I was shocked. Presents hiding, practically, in plain sight. The woman was a master of Christmas espionage.

In fact, her present barrel trick was just the start of her holiday genius. There was also the year that my mom created gift bags, a category that did not *yet* exist in the gift-giving industry. I know for anyone young reading this, that seems insane, but it is true. Gift wrap was for many years our only option. It was a dark time.

Then, my mother unexpectedly created the entire category of the gift bag. I could have been an heiress. I could have owned a jet. But, no...that inheritance was not to be realized because my mother did not even know that she had stumbled upon an industry-changing invention in 1983 when she dreamed up the idea of the gift bag.

Exhausted from wrapping presents at midnight, my mother decided she needed a new plan. She had hours of wrapping ahead of her. She wanted to outright boycott the entire endeavor but knew doing so would crush the souls of my brother and me. So, with my father — her "helper" — sleeping on the family room floor, cradling a tape dispenser in his hands, my mother hatched an idea. She stood up, stepped over my father, and went to the basement steps, where she grabbed all the paper grocery store bags we had hoarded.

She returned to the family room floor, flipped over the second barrel, and started placing gifts in bags. It took less than five minutes. She was giddy at the pace. When she was finished, however, she stepped back and realized that she was staring at a wall of IGA grocery store logos.

"Well, that won't do," she said aloud.

"Are we done wrapping yet?" my dad asked from the floor, still half asleep.

"Go to bed, Armin," my mom said flatly as she began cutting large rectangles of wrapping paper.

"I'm helping you wrap," he said defensively, rolling over onto his back and crushing a bolt of ribbon in the process.

Shaking her head at my father, my mom began to fold each of the large swathes of paper in half so that she could, then, drape one over each bag to cover the logo.

The result was stunning. The tree was surrounded by a swirl of craft paper and ribbon. She stared at her work and concluded that she needed to keep the gift wrap logo covers in place somehow, so she began taping them down. After two bags, however, she realized that approach was too labor intensive. So, she went to the desk, retrieved the stapler, and stapled the bags shut with the paper now held firmly in place.

The next morning, we rushed downstairs at 6 a.m., and found the tree surrounded by decorative bags. It was so gorgeous, I gasped. I had never seen anything like it.

As I shredded my fourth bag pulling out the Strawberry Shortcake tea set that was inside, I told my mom, "These bags are genius. Someone should sell them."

My father immediately scoffed and dismissed the idea. "I had to take pliers to get two staples outta my foot already. I'm bleeding like a stuck pig over here. I don't think anyone's using these bags without a tetanus shot on hand."

If only my mother had considered printing the pattern on the paper. Had she done that...well, I would have been an heiress, now writing this book from Richard Branson's island.

Of course, there was also the time that I helped my mother decorate the shelves and front window of the clothing boutique she and a partner owned. I arrived to work — where I was a part-time sales associate — only to find her stacking four piles of boxes next to four large bolts of wrapping paper.

"Put that can of RC down," she instructed. "Each of these boxes has a pre-determined spot on the shelves." She gestured above us to the pine-laden displays overhead. "I've already figured out what goes where and weighted each box so they'll stand properly on the shelves. All you have to do is wrap them. I put the wrapping paper bolt next to the corresponding pile. Don't get them mixed up. I know what pattern goes where, but just in case, write the number from each box on the back of each wrapped present. Don't forget that they all need ribbon. Make them pretty."

I spent two days wrapping all the boxes, tying each one with elaborate ribbon bows and adding sprigs of pine or peppermint canes with floral wire. My fingers were so chapped and dry that I bled on at least three of the boxes. When I was finished, I had a stack of ivory with red holly in group one. Group two was green plaid. Three was silver snowflakes. And four was Merry & Bright.

Together, my mother and I placed the wrapped packages around the store and in the front window, putting each box back right where she said it should go. She even had a hand drawn map with her notes for us to follow. When we were finished, the store looked gorgeous, punctuated by the elaborately wrapped boxes.

"It looks like Lazarus in here," I said, admiring my work.

"No kidding," my mom said. To this very day, a department store circa 1989 remains my desired effect for every holiday display I design in my own home, all thanks to the Lazarus perfume counter, my mother, and her boutique-decorating capabilities.

On Christmas morning at our house, I ran downstairs expecting to find a mismatch of wrapped presents surrounding the tree. I was shocked, however, to find instead the stacks of gifts I had wrapped for my mother's store.

"What's going on?" I asked.

My mother sat down on our nearly-new loveseat — bought at Lazarus, I might add — with her cup of black coffee in hand and said, "Kristin, you're the ivory with holly, your dad is green plaid, and Brian, you're merry & bright."

"Wait, I wrapped all of our presents?"

She yawned, "You sure did."

My mother is a pioneer.

Not only that, but we've always been *that* family, the one that makes Christmas fun by offering up gift directives like, "Group present. Everyone opens together. Love, Prancer" or "Don't open until your mom says you can. Love, Rudolph"

So, when my oma came over to me at her house that year and put her hand on my shoulder to issue her Christmas instructions, I thought nothing of it.

"This pile goes first," she said, pointing to a stack of presents directly to my right. "And this stack goes last," she added placing her hand atop a second pile of gifts to my left.

Each time my turn came, I pulled from the first stack, just as she had directed. One by one, I whittled away at that first pile. A scarf, homemade pickles, a knit hat, and then a pair of Isotoner gloves.

When the first pile was unwrapped, I turned to the second, lifting the top present from the stack onto my lap.

As my dad and brother continued opening video games, flannel shirts, and whiskey filled chocolates, I began opening every single item that had previously been gifted to me by grandmother and that I had sold at the garage sale.

First came the cat tea kettle. Then came the haunted cat lamp. Next was the hellscape of the Santa cat. All in total I opened eleven items that were originally gifts she and my grandfather had given to me in years past, each one sold at my parent's family garage sale — half of which I had, honestly, forgotten were gifts from them in the first place.

The last present in the stack came with a card that read: *I can't imagine you really wanted to get rid of the things we gave you. So, here they are coming back to you. Fröhliche Weihnachten! Love Oma and Opa*

I looked up to see her smiling at me from across the room. "Now we just have to get that trunk back, don't we?" she asked.

My Oma, like every great mob boss, was always good at the long con.

The next week, I asked my friend to take pictures of the trunk as a proof of life. I then sent those pictures to my oma with a note that read, "The trunk's back home...right where she belongs. Love, Kristin"

Of course, my oma didn't believe me for a second that the trunk was *actually* at my house. The second she had opened the envelope, she called me.

"Where did you put it? In what room?"

Without even an ounce of hesitation, I answered, "It's in my living room. I'm looking at it right now."

"Hmmmm," she intoned over the phone.

"You're free to come and visit anytime. See it for yourself, or if you want to take it back home with you, you can," I offered.

Of course, I knew she wouldn't come to Chicago. This was the same woman who drove from Ohio to Niagara Falls and back in the same day with the explanation of, "Opa doesn't love the way restaurants make their potatoes."

"We promised it to our neighbors," she said, attempting to call my bluff.

So, I called her bluff right back.

"Well, give *me* their number. Maybe I can call them and tell them I want to keep it. Ask them if they'll understand?"

There was a long pause and then, "No, it's okay. As long as you have it."

Each time we spoke, she asked about that trunk, and each time she did I sent her a picture. The trunk decked out for the holidays. The trunk with a TV on it. The trunk as a bedside table. This was, of course, a ruse I had to keep up until the bitter end of her life.

In fact, when she died, I told my dad, "You picked a really beautiful coffin. She would have loved the whole service," I told him on the drive home.

He solemnly nodded his head, "I'm glad. I think so, too."

"I just think," I told him, eyeing him in the rearview mirror of the car, "I could have saved you a lot of money if you had just let me snap her in half and bury her in that trunk."

"Kristin Ann!" my dad shouted. "That is not funny."

"Uhhhh, it's kind of funny Dad," I said with a smile.

I knew he wanted to be outraged. This was, after all, his mother, a woman he loved very much. And in my own way, I loved her too. But, at the end of the day, even he had to laugh and admit, "She *just* couldn't let go of that damn trunk, could she?"

"No," I said, howling with laughter.

Of all the lessons I learned from my Oma, good and bad, I consider my dedication to the long con to be the most useful. I know that sounds negative, and in the wrong hands it certainly can be. But I choose to use this power for good and not evil.

I have simply learned that in business and in life, sometimes we have to wait one another out...sometimes we have to wait ourselves out...because everything is revealed. Intentions. Agendas. Mistruths. Abundance. It is all seen, eventually. Yet, we can't impose reveals on anyone else, nor can we alter the divine timing of our lives.

We all have those friends who are in the wrong relationship, who are certain they are not worthy of their dreams, who are telling us they can't take the risk on that job due to their responsibilities...heck, we've all been that person from time to time. Some of us might even be that person right now.

Here's the thing, though, try as we might to make them believe or force them to see that none of that is true, they won't and can't see that reveal until it is timed for them.

It's sort of in keeping with the quote, "when the student is ready, the teacher will appear." It's the idea that when the timing is right, we are finally able to receive the information, data, or awakening we need.

I've come to believe that our longest con is the one we are pulling on ourselves, or at least that's how it's been for me.

Each time we spin these narratives or create these emotional alibis, we are potentially conning ourselves into and out of perspectives that may or may not be real — may or may not serve us.

The truth is, we are each capable of immense change. No story is so far along that we can't exit out of it and begin anew entirely. There is no expiration date on our potential, dictating that we must now forfeit the possibilities of our lives.

Most importantly, who we are is not *fated*. It is *formulated* in our brains, beliefs, and behaviors.

Change any one of those and our world not only shifts, it cracks wide open in unimaginable and unprecedented ways.

All this stuff we tell ourselves: "My family is counting on me." "My kids won't be happy if I do it." "It's too late to make that into in a business." "I'm not good enough."

It's all a part of the con.

So, I say if we are going to con ourselves...because I know we all are...we all do...then we ought to choose the longest and hardest con of them all — to believe we are worthy of the love, the dream, and the possibility we are so deeply afraid that we do not deserve.

ELEVEN

Hit and Run

"Are you getting divorced?" I asked my mom as she angrily stormed up our narrow staircase and stepped over me on the landing.

"What are you even doing up? You should be in bed," she huffed.

She had a valid point. She had hugged me well over an hour before and had sent me off to bed. But, as was often the case on Mondays, I had promptly sneaked out of my room and tip-toed to our landing to secretly watch *Kate & Allie* over her shoulder.

That landing was my spot and not just for *Kate & Allie*. I would creep down the stairs at least twice a week, lying on the pine green carpeting of our staircase landing to watch television long after I was already meant to be in bed.

It wasn't a comfortable spot by any means. To get a bird's eye view of the television, I had to position myself flush with the step above the landing and crane my neck out over the step below the landing. That position was the only way I could then get my eyes to line up between the slats of wood in our banister. Any other position meant my whole body would be visible on the staircase below.

Of course, lying there meant that I was then forced to hold this position the entire time I watched. Thank goodness there was no fast forward in the 80s. I had the blessing of commercials to rest my neck. Without *that* I would have been the very first case of tech neck ever documented in the United States.

There were plenty of nights, however, after I'd been there for about ten minutes that my mother would threaten, "You have three seconds to get back in bed or you're grounded."

"How'd you even know I was here?" I'd whine. "You didn't even turn around."

"I don't have to turn around. I have eyes in the back of my head."

Naturally, I believed her. I had years of data where she'd caught me doing something in the backseat without even taking her eyes off the road.

What I never realized was that from her vantage point on the sofa she could see my reflection in the window across from her. She didn't need to turn around. To be fair, though, there were many nights when she didn't notice me there at all, and I'd make it through every delicious Julia Sugarbaker monologue in *Designing Women*.

On those nights, I thought I'd outfoxed her only to wake up as she was carrying me upstairs to bed *after* I'd fallen asleep on the stairs. I'd mumble, "I was just coming down for water," but we both knew the jig was up. I'd been caught red-handed. I'm not as smooth a criminal as I would have hoped.

Tonight, however, the TV was off. Even if it had been on, *Kate and Allie* would have been drowned out by my parents' fighting.

As I lay stiff as a board on our stairsteps listening to them shout, I realized they'd been arguing a lot lately. And, even when they weren't fighting, the air still popped and sizzled with resentment.

My mother came flying around the corner and bounded up the steps so fast that I didn't even have a second to react. She was moving at such a fast clip that she startled both of us before I could even consider running back to bed. She took a giant leap over the landing to avoid stepping on top of me.

"Kristin!" she said breathless. "Get back to bed."

"Are you and dad getting a divorce?" I asked.

She hoovered over me as I lay on my back staring up at her, the bright neon pink of my JEM nightgown clashing with our evergreen carpet.

She paused for a moment, obviously pondering my emotional health and psychological well-being before giving the careful reply of, "Don't worry. We can't afford a divorce. Now go to bed."

I could feel my lower lip start to quiver. I smashed my hair back off my forehead with the forearm of my nightgown as I trudged up the steps to my bedroom.

Back in bed, I fought against the tears that rested on the rims of my eyes and stared out across the roof of our front porch to the streetlamp just beyond.

Behind me, in the recesses of our upstairs, I heard my mother slam the medicine cabinet before angrily rooting around in the bathroom cupboard. She only halted her mad search through the closet to shout random declarations and obscenities down the steps at my father.

"Keep yelling, Jan!" I heard my dad shout back as he passed the bathroom in the hall on his way up. "I don't think you woke up the entire neighborhood just yet."

I heard their bedroom door slam shut and an eerie quiet settled over the house.

I felt my mom in the doorway before she spoke.

"I shouldn't have said that," she offered quietly.

"Is it true?" I demanded.

She didn't answer. A second later I felt my bed sag as she sat on the edge of the mattress. She pulled the corner of my seafoam green and mauve comforter up over my shoulder and tucked it under my chin.

"What's *true* is that grown-ups don't always see eye to eye. Your father is driving me nuts right now, but as mad as I am at him, I love our family more. So, we'll fix this."

I rolled over to look at her. "And, what happens when you make more money?"

She barked out a wheezing laugh and said flatly, "That's not gonna happen."

Then she stood and closed my bedroom door as she walked back out to go to bed. Not exactly the warm fuzzy assurance I was looking for, but then my mother, a Cancer, never really did warm fuzzy.

She was and is what she would refer to as a realist. I, however, have affectionately come to re-classify her version of realism as borderline pessimism disorder. This is, of course, not a clinical diagnosis, just what I taunt her with whenever she tries to sell me on her realism jag.

Although, I do now realize that the three cardinal rules my mom raised me under were all squarely rooted in her brand of realism, and, looking back, I 100% agree with each one of them.

"First, I hate when people use baby talk," she'd informed me just prior to my inaugural babysitting gig. "You can't expect a kid to cope with whatever life gives 'em unless they've been taught the words to talk about it. So call everything exactly *what* it is and *as* it is. Don't discount things by underselling them with babble. If a kid needs food, you better have taught them how to say they're hungry. Give them the words to communicate what it is that they need. A person can only ask *for* what they've been taught *the words for*. And never call your *vagina* anything but a *vagina*. Everyone's already trying to lessen what it is to be a woman. Don't make it easier to undermine us all by calling one of the most significant parts of yourself something horrific like a wooby. It's tacky."

Later came this lesson:

"Don't ever let anyone tell you what you can and can't do — except for me." She cocked one eyebrow to punctuate her joke. "But, seriously, you have to live your life for you. No one else. People always say to put your marriage first or your kids first or God first. I'm here to tell you, *you* go to the front of your own line. People who aren't living for themselves end up halved or quartered. But when you live for *you* first, you are whole, and whole has more to give."

Of course, one of the great sadnesses for my mother is that she, herself, didn't follow rule number two. I had my suspicions about her adherence to her own second rule because each time she'd say, "You go first. First has more to give," I'd notice that my mother never went first. She had mapped her life the opposite way. Her start as a mom was one made of sacrifice and the dismissal of her own dreams...a hunch my grandmother, her beloved mother, confirmed for me.

"You know your mother wanted be an artist, right?" my gramma had randomly said to me as we sat in her sunny, pink living room watching *Murder She Wrote*. I loved that living room, and I loved dearly my mom's mother.

"No," I shook my head.

"Yea, she sure did, and she could have been a great one. I think it's why your mom is so adamant that you go out in the world and be exactly who you want to be. I'll never forget. She told me she was applying to art school when she was a senior in high school."

"Really?"

My gramma nodded her head. "She's very talented, your mother. She gets it from me, you know?" She smiled in my direction.

I smiled in return. She was right. My mom did get her creativity from my gramma, her mother, and I got mine from the both of them.

"She came home from school as proud as a peacock on the day she decided she was going to apply. I had never seen her carry herself that way. She was...," I watched my gramma stare out her front window as if searching for a word in that memory, "...*taller*. She was taller. I, of course, had told her, her whole life how good she was, but she never believed me. But once this idea was set, once she had made up her mind to apply...well, she was just different. She had this air about her. For weeks her shoulders squared up differently. She was confident and it looked good on her. And then suddenly...POOF...she came home from school and said she was going to secretarial college instead. No more art school."

"Why?" I asked.

"My question exactly, I asked her, *'Jan, what are you talking about? You want to go to art school'*, but she wouldn't have it. She wouldn't discuss it with me. She said her mind was made up. I was sick over it. And all that height she'd gotten from *choosing* herself...it was gone. It just left her."

"So, what did you do?"

"I went to the school. I asked the guidance counselor. I said, *'What do you think happened? What caused this? Why is Jan suddenly intent on pursuing secretarial work?'*"

"And what did the counselor say?"

"That *horrible* woman," my grandmother peered back out the window, staring into the memory of that school guidance counselor's office. "The guidance counselor told me that *she* had told Jan to be smart. *'I asked Jan,' she said, 'don't you think it's selfish of you to go to art school? Your parents don't have enough money for you to just throw it all away and that's what you would be doing as their daughter if you went to art school...wasting their money.'"* My grandmother turned toward me. "She admitted that to me. I was gob smacked."

"What did you say when the counselor told you that?"

"I was so mad I could have spit nails. I told her she had no right to take that from my daughter. I told her that Jan was meant to be an artist...*was* an artist...*is* an artist. I asked her, *'How dare you take that from my daughter?'"*

"And what did *she* say?"

"Nothing. She just looked at me like I had slapped her. I think she was shocked that I would want my daughter to pursue art," my grandmother paused and turned to look back out the window, getting one last look at that traitorous guidance counselor before returning her gaze to me. "You know, it was a different time....then. Women didn't work like they do now. Most people wouldn't have wanted their daughters to go to art school, I guess. But I'm not most people, am I?"

"Obviously," I concurred, smiling broadly at my gramma. "So, *what* did you do?"

"Well, I went home, and I told your mom she was going to that art school, end of conversation. But she refused. She's very stubborn, your mother."

"I know. I think she gets that from you, too." I smiled.

My gramma laughed. "You're probably right."

I watched as she looked back toward the memory that seemed to be standing just on the other side of her picture window, a frame that only she could see. She then, slowly, wiped a tear away from her eyes before turning back to me.

"Don't ever let anyone tell you that *you* don't get your dreams, Kristin. You take all that moxie you have, and you put it to use. Because when you don't, the world misses out on all that you have to give it. Just like they missed out on my Jan."

I still encourage my mom every chance I get to be the writer and artist she was meant to be. I see that part of her emerge more and more each year as I watch her bravely lean into the third rule she demanded that I live by:

"Trust your gut, Kristin, and don't ever apologize for it because at the end of the day you don't owe people as much as you think you do."

We were headed across town to go back-to-school shopping. It wasn't the first time my mom had told me some version of that on one of our many car conversations.

As a sidenote, I've found that if you want to have a good chat with someone, drive somewhere together. Sing. Laugh. Spill the tea. There's something about an open road that invites an open dialogue. You can't go two different directions when you're in the same car. Wherever you're going, you're going there together, and you're going to talk about it.

What I saw as I got older was that, even if my mom hadn't always followed her dreams, she *had* always followed her gut. I watched her follow her instincts on everything from the amount of ketchup to put in the meatloaf to parenting like her declaration when I was nine....

"Everyone into the basement!" she shouted at us as she breezed through our small kitchen one crisp spring morning. When none of us moved, she barked, "Now!"

My dad, brother, and I, all stood, aware no good could come from our being summoned to the basement. Regardless, we dutifully followed her in a single file line down the uneven staircase into our damp basement. Once downstairs, my father and brother stooped down to avoid hitting their heads on the low ceiling, and the trio of us gathered around her in a horseshoe of sorts by the washer and dryer.

"See this," my mom said, pointing at the washer. "This is a washing machine. And *this*," she said gesturing at the machine directly to its right like Vanna White would point to a letter, "is a dryer."

We stared at her, unblinking.

"Look alive, People," she clapped, "nod if you understand me."

The three of us nodded our heads in unison.

"Goooood. Now, this...*this*, is detergent." She held up a half empty bottle of Wisk and shook it in front of us. "And just for good measure, this is fabric softener for the washer, and these are the sheets for the dryer," she now juggled all three items in her hands. "Are you still with me?" she questioned.

We nodded again.

"Perfect. Moving on. This is the lint trap. You empty it after each load, okay?"

She looked back at us again to gauge our understanding.

"Janet, we know how to do the laundry," my father interrupted her, with an almost patronizing tone.

"Yes," my mom replied supportively. "You are correct. Of course you know how to do laundry," she concurred.

My father shrugged his shoulders and shook his head as if nonverbally saying, "See we agree with one another."

But then she paused. "It's just that for people who *know* how to do the laundry, you seem to be doing very little of it around here."

A chill swooped in across the already cold basement. This is where we all saw the other shoe start to drop.

"What I think you *actually* know how to do is to wait for *me* to do the laundry."

She stared at us awaiting our admission of this egregious truth. We remained frozen.

"Because in this house, I seem to be the only one *actually* doing the laundry. And not just that, now it seems that I'm the only one who knows how to pick your clothes up off the floor, put them in the hamper, bring them downstairs, and eventually wash them. Am I right? Because, when I say it out loud, it rings true to me."

As far as a prosecution went, she seemed to be making an airtight case.

She stared us down, her prey. We didn't move. We had seen enough Jack Hanna during Saturday morning cartoons to know that when you are trapped in a basement with an angry leopard, you remain still.

So, she continued. "I guess, what I'm hoping to now see is you *actually* doing this laundry you say you know to do."

She stared at my father. "Well, that seems fair," he admitted.

She then looked to my brother and then on to me for the same acknowledgement. We gave it.

"Good. I'm glad we're on the same page, because from this moment forward, I will no longer be doing *any* laundry in this house. I am going to start behaving like you, where I just wait for someone else to do the laundry. So, I am done with the piles of clothes you throw down the basement steps for *me* to sort. I am done with you reminding me that you need PJs. I am done with folding laundry that you don't put away. I am just done. So, I will not be washing lights. I will not be doing a load of darks. You want clean underwear? You will do it yourself, or you will go to school or work naked. Understood?"

We each gave a solemn nod.

"Good," she said. "To christen your new ship, the SOS laundry, here is my first load of darks for you. Enjoy." With that, she shoved a round plastic laundry basket filled with her clothes into my father's arms and disappeared upstairs.

Once she was gone, the three of *us* reacted the only way humanly possible. We immediately turned on one another, blaming each other, and verbally attacking one another for our current circumstance.

"This is all your fault!" I shouted at my brother.

"Me?" he argued back. "I don't think so!"

As we argued, my father hurled at me, "What did you do, Kristin?"

"How is this my fault?" I defended. "I *always* put my laundry away."

"You're such a liar," my brother accused.

"Yea, well she didn't just freak out over nothing!" I shouted back. "You're the one who left your stack of clothes on the table for a whole week, even though she told you each day to take 'em upstairs!" I yelled back at him.

"I'd say less arguing and more sorting," my mother chirped down from the kitchen doorway above.

My dad let out a dramatic sigh. "Knock it off, the both of you. Just do what your mother says, already." He held out the basket of laundry for either my brother or me to take. We, of course, dodged him entirely and raced upstairs, leaving my dad to handle what would be the first load of many loads of laundry for the rest of our lives.

In some ways, you could argue my mother's strike continues until this very day. Yes, she does laundry again, but at the same time, she never actually declared her strike over. We live under the constant threat of her walking off the assembly line again.

It seems her basement declaration still stands. What is different is that *we* acclimated to her new terms. She told me years later, "I'm no fool. When none of you complained, I kept my mouth shut. I wasn't going to go begging to be your laundromat once again."

I was only nine when my mother officially exited the spin cycle that is the family wash. She told me that even she wondered at the time, *'Is Kristin too young to be doing all her own laundry, already?'*

But she followed her gut, and it said I would figure it out and *probably* be all the more respectful and responsible for it.

Her gut was right. Intuition is powerful that way.

When I was eleven, I actually asked her about intuition.

We were on the way home from visiting my mom's side of the family, and as was usually the case, we had stayed longer than expected and we were driving along a country road in the pitch black of night.

As we drove, we listened to a late-night radio show about relationships. Different callers dialed in to share their stories of love and heartache and ask for song dedications to go along with their tales of woe.

After about the tenth caller, I asked my mom, "Do you ever know stuff that no one taught you, but somehow you just know it?"

My mom turned down the radio, "Like what? Facts?" she asked.

"Maybe...but more like *things* about situations or topics or even people that no one told you? You just *know* the answer. And even if they go a different route, in the end, it turns out that you were right."

She considered this for a moment. "Does that happen to you?" she asked as she peered at me in the rearview mirror.

I nodded. "I think so."

"Like what?" she asked.

"I don't know, just *things*...what to do about something or you just know something about someone...maybe something they don't even know about themselves. You just feel it."

"Hmmm," she hummed. "Well, that's your intuition and if yours is talking to you *that* way, that's pretty darn special. You need to hold onto that, for sure. I think that's like a superpower. If you can do that, you have this amazing gift that will probably be one of your biggest assets in life. Whatever you do, don't let anyone tell you not to listen to that part of you. Always trust it."

"Okay," I said, and with that my mother turned the radio back up just as the host gave a shout out to Kenny and Ang on their tenth anniversary.

My mom was right. That skill has informed every area of my life. It's my ace in the hole, my rabbit out of the hat.

I don't always trust myself, but I *always* trust my intuition.

I think it's an important distinction because there is a story we tell ourselves *about ourselves* in our own brains. That tale we are spinning doesn't always serve us. But our instinct comes from a different place, a more true place, a more trusted place when we hone it.

Our brain might say all kinds of awful things to us, but our intuition — when strengthened — is our biggest truth-sayer. Intuition wants us to leap, run, and rise. Not only that it is our truest connection to the Universe and the power we hold as humans.

Of course, my mom (and dad) taught me many more life
lessons. Some of which — like my mother's top three rules
— were intended. Others, like the fact that my mom
cannot admit when she is wrong to save her own life, were
not.

Case and point, my mom once ran over my dad with our
family car. To this day, hand to Bible, she will still defend
the truth that it was not her fault.

"How can it be *my* fault when you told me to go?" my mom
asks each time the topic comes up. "You got out of the car
to wipe the snow off the windshield. You motioned for me
to move. I did. Where is the problem in that?"

My dad's response is always the same and is always sound.
"The problem is, *Jan*, that you ran me over with our car."

"Don't be dramatic, Armin. It was just your feet, and you
told me to go. So I did."

"Go?! I motioned for you to turn on the windshield
wipers. Why in our tiny carport would I motion for you to
drive backwards?"

"I asked myself the very same thing when you did it," my
mother always points out as if this fact still astounds her.

The best part about the entire scene was that my brother
and I were in the backseat for the whole incident. We had
just loaded into the car to drive to our family

Thanksgiving. Snow had come early, and our tiny, one car garage could only fit one vehicle. Our maroon Chevette with its bright orange pinstripe — the hatchback we had just proudly purchased — was designated to park in the attached patio that had been appropriated as a carport. The patio had a roof, but as was the case with any snow or freezing rain, the car's windshield was entirely exposed and thus covered with ice. It had been pelted in snow.

On the day in question, my dad had hopped out of the car to clean off the windshield for my mother who was driving. Because of the carport's size, he opted not to squeeze in between the wall and the vehicle. Instead, he stood on the passenger side and leaned way into the car, stretching across the hood to wipe the driver side without walking around — hence, why his feet were tucked under the car.

As he swept the snow away, I watched it flutter up into the air before floating into the open passenger door and showering me with a fine mist of cold snow in the backseat. Then he motioned. I knew it was for the windshield wipers, but I watched as my mother put the car in reverse. When she backed up, the nearly 3,000-pound car drove up and over my father's feet. He buckled, then screamed so loudly that we all screamed inside the car along with him. He then smacked his hands down on the windshield with such force that my mother thought she might still be on top of his feet. In a panic she threw the car into drive and drove forward, driving back over his feet for a second time.

My father screamed again. So, naturally, we did, too inside the car. Freaked out, my mom slammed the car back into park and we lurched forward in our seats. Stunned my father fell forward and lay draped across the hood.

"Is he dead?" I asked.

"Of course not," my mother assured me.

We stared at him through the windshield. He didn't move, so my mother gently honked the horn. My dad jolted upright.

"What are you doing to me?" my dad shouted through the windshield.

We watched as my father stood and then staggered back, catching himself on the passenger door. He then clung to it for dear life before pulling himself back up. Hobbled, he limped around the door and fell into the front seat.

"Damnit Janet! What in the hell are you doing? You just ran me over....twice!"

"I did not!" my mother exclaimed.

"You did, too!" he shouted back.

"Well, you motioned for me to drive," my mother defended.

My dad spun in his seat to look at her. "No, I motioned for you to turn on the windshield wipers."

The realization of his words and the recollection of his gesture, hit my mother. As it dawned on her, we watched her process her mistake. A normal person would have immediately led with an apology, but not my mom. She, instead, went with, "Well you should have been more clear, Armin."

My dad's reaction was just to slump forward in his seat and rest his head against the glove box. "I think my feet are broken," he said, weakly.

"As in you need to go to the hospital?" my mother asked.

"I don't know," my dad said, his voice muffled by the dashboard.

We all stared at him, holding our breath.

"How do you know if your feet are broken?" he asked quietly.

"Well, I would think for starters you wouldn't have been able to walk on them to get back in the car," my mom offered.

My dad didn't move. He just sat motionless, his head resting on the car's vinyl.

"Armin?" my mom prodded.

"Don't talk to me, Janet. I need one God Damn minute. Can I have that, or do you want to run me over for a third time?"

My mom looked over her shoulder at me as I sat in the backseat. She shook her head and rolled her eyes. "You're so dramatic," she began.

"Dramatic?" my dad cut her off. "Okay, I'll hit you, and *you* tell me if I'm being dramatic."

"Okay," my mom conceded, putting her hands up in surrender. "Take a beat."

We sat perfectly still watching to see what my dad would do next, when my mother broke the silence in the car. "From where I sit, you have two choices Armin, okay?"

My dad looked up at my mom, awaiting his options.

"You can stay here with *maybe* broken feet and frozen pizza alone, or you can go with *maybe* broken feet to Thanksgiving dinner and eat pumpkin pie with everyone else."

My father stared at her in disbelief. "Is that *really* all you have to say?" he asked.

My mother peered into the back seat, looking at me, and then returned her gaze to my father. I could see her considering what he might be wanting from her. She then said, "Well I guess you could *also* have pecan pie."

"Aren't you even going to say you're sorry, Janet?" my dad asked with outrage.

"I'm sorry," she said, "but in my defense you motioned for me to drive. You have to admit that."

"I want you to know that I am only staying in this car because I cannot handle the idea of walking all the way to the front door right now," my dad threatened.

"Well, great, pie it is," my mom said as she put the car in reverse.

I have realized over the years from watching my parents that relationships of every kind — be it spouses, boyfriends, girlfriends, friends, or coworkers — always benefit when we *really* see the people with whom we are in the relationship.

S*eeing* people means seeing the good and the bad character traits they have. It means seeing their light and their shade. Successful relationships can only be navigated when you see both. Otherwise, you're just driving in the dark and someone is bound to get run over when you do that. Just ask my father.

I've learned that we tend to overstate the good because that's what we fall in love with, and we try to dismantle or change the bad.

My parents showed me that in partnership there is a certain amount of surrender.

I think surrendering gets a bad rap. We speak of it in only negative terms. We are Braveheart on the horse, with our swords raised high above our heads shouting, "...they may take our lives, but they will never take our freedom...," as if freedom means bending what we do not like in others to *our* will and breaking them of the core character traits that don't serve *us*.

I instead lived in a house, where my parents openly spoke about the emotional limits that were hardwired into who we are. My mom can't admit she is wrong. My dad hates change of any kind; I'm talking if you reverse the way we walk through the grocery store he falls apart.

I am not good at giving people their space in conflict. I want to sort it out, *now*, and move on. My mom despises that in me. She has said to me at least three times in my life, "You will not hold me hostage to your psychological timeline." She's not wrong. I can be an emotional terrorist who just wants you to talk about your shit or our conflict so we can all move past it.

My brother for his big heart can be emotionally ambivalent when a situation doesn't serve him.

Point is, we have all come to understand what we love about one other *and* what we would, perhaps, change about each other. Obviously, the good parts are easy. But, what about the *less* good? To me, *those* traits feel like a comment box on the wall of a giant fast-food chain. Sure, we could fill out a card and drop it inside, but I'm not so sure in the grand scheme of things *we're* actually going to change much by doing so. Much like we can't control when a favorite gordita comes back on the menu, we *also* can't control the character traits of other humans. We just have to order the Burrito Supreme and cope with it.

At the end of the day, though, I believe there is beauty in loving people not for who we want them to be but for who they *are*...ourselves included. And that's just a little lesson, I learned from my mam

IN CLOSING

So where does all this leave us?

Well, when I was a junior in high school, I told my parents that the window AC unit in my bedroom was making noises.

"What do you mean *making* noises?" my dad asked, immediately alarmed. "What kind of noises? Did you do something to it?"

Police officers will tell you it's always the husband. My dad's investigative style was more that whoever reported the problem was probably the perp.

"I didn't do anything," I defended. "It's ancient. It's probably just futzing out."

Not appeased by my diagnosis, my father threw down the dish towel he was holding and immediately headed for the stairs. "Let's go see what you did," he surmised.

I followed him in hot pursuit up the staircase to our wood-paneled second floor where my bedroom was located. Each summer it was a hotbox up there. Without an AC unit, there was no hope for my being able to sleep on the second floor between June, July, and August.

"I'm not buying a new one if you already broke this one," he said as we rounded the top of the staircase." I just put it in this week, Kristin."

"I didn't break it. I just turned it on."

"You probably twisted the knob too far, didn't you? That's probably what you did," he accused.

I rolled my eyes at him.

He swung open the door to my bedroom and cold air rushed toward us. He did that thing that all dads do; he put up his hand to feel the cool air. "It's cold in here. What are you talking about? It works." He turned to face me.

"I didn't say it didn't work. I *said* it's making noises."

My dad went over to the window and knelt directly in front of the unit. I started to speak but he silenced me by raising his hand in my direction. Perfectly still, he listened.

"I don't hear anything. What kind of noises was it making?"

"I don't know," I shrugged, "noises."

"Well, that's super helpful," he taunted.

"Clangs...chirps," I added.

"Well, it's not making any noises now. Problem solved," he joked. He then stood and headed for the door, adding, "When the noises come back, call me. Until then try not to make more problems, that we can't afford to fix, okay?"

"Would you get out already?" I chided.

For weeks, he and I had this routine where I'd scream down the steps, "It's happening!" and my dad would run upstairs, only to kneel in front of a perfectly quiet AC unit.

"Maybe tomorrow it'll finally be broken in front of someone other than just you," he'd tease.

After a month, I stopped shouting for my dad, altogether, but that didn't stop him from heckling me. "How's that *broken* AC, still cranking out that cool air for ya?"

By the time fall rolled around, I had outright started ignoring the noises. Each time they bubbled out, I'd turn up my headphones and do my best to drown out the sounds.

And, then summer was over.

"Your mom wants us to take all the air conditioners out this weekend," my dad informed me as I packed my backpack for school. "We're late. It's already mid-September. We can't put it off another weekend, okay?"

I ignored him. "Okay?" he shouted again.

"Fine," I said

"Good, Saturday morning before you go to work. It's a date," he said.

First thing Saturday my dad was raring to go. I had never been on AC install or removal duty before. As far as I knew, it was a job my dad and brother took care of each year, but my brother was away at college, now, so that meant I was left holding the bag.

First, we completed the living room, then the den, and finally my parents' room. In less than an hour the downstairs was complete, with all three of the first floor ACs now carefully resting on bricks in the basement.

We moved upstairs.

I grimaced under the weight of the AC unit in my brother's bedroom. "Why did you even put an AC in Brian's room, this year?" I asked as I hauled the hundred-pound AC unit forward from the window. "He didn't even come home this summer. He stayed in Cleveland, working at the radio station."

"Your mother told me to put it in the window."

"Why didn't you tell her no?" I argued.

"Why don't *you* tell her no?" my dad rebutted.

As we slowly walked down the hall my dad observed, "We should have started with the two upstairs. They're the heaviest. We should have gotten 'em out of the way first."

"Hold on," I commanded as we turned to navigate what would be our first flight of steps. "You're pushing me," I warned as I precariously walked backwards down the staircase.

"This is killing my back," my dad whined. "You have to go faster."

"I can't," I shouted.

We argued more while removing the one AC unit in my brother's room than we had in all three of the units on the first floor. And, believe me, we had argued during *each* of those as well. At one point in the den, I had said to my father, "It would be less work for me to murder you and hide your body than it is to deal with these air conditioners. We need central air."

"You gonna pay for it?" he had replied.

As we trudged back up the steps from the basement, to tackle the last man standing — the AC unit in my bedroom — my dad tried his best to give us a pep talk, "Last one. We got this," he chirped, clapping his hands.

"Can you fucking not?" I chided. *I was a real dream as a teenager.*

"First of all, language," my dad warned, "Second of all, you're no fun," he teased.

"Can we just go already?" I demanded as we stood in my room.

"Hold on," my dad said assessing my bedroom air conditioner. "We need a plan for this one."

"Isn't it the same we've had for all the others we've done? Open the window. Remove the AC. Carry it downstairs," I patronized in the "*duh*" tone of voice every parent loves.

"No, it's not that *easy*," my dad warned. "For your information, this one weighs 300lbs. It's so heavy, we had to screw it into the window." He pointed to the bolts. "Not only that the tension on the window sash doesn't work. The second we pull it out, the window's going to slam down and the glass is gonna break."

I looked at the broken sash my dad was referring to, "So now what?" I asked.

"Let me think," my dad said assessing the situation. He then grabbed my shoulders and maneuvered me to the left of the window. He stepped back and pantomimed some moves as if he were choreographing the removal himself. As he moved through the room with an invisible AC in his arms, he muttered to himself. Suddenly he said aloud, "No, that can't work. You have to go here." He then moved me to the right of the window.

"And what am I doing *here*?"

He mapped out our game plan for the both of us. "First, I'll unscrew the bolts."

I nodded.

"Then I'm going to tip the AC unit forward."

I nodded again.

"When I tip the AC *forward*, you have to get your fingers under the pane and raise it up...JUST A BIT...so that I can get the unit *through* the window into the room a smidge. Then you'll quickly but *carefully* close the window. Don't let it slam shut," he warned, "then jump to help me get the unit on the ground. Got it?" he asked.

"I guess so."

He arched an eyebrow at me.

"Yes, I got it," I said, flatly

"Okay, first, plastic...." I watched as my dad laid garbage bags on the floor to protect the carpet. He then studied his work, clapped his hands, and turned to me. "Ready?" he asked.

"I guess so."

He sagged his shoulders in defeat.

"Yes, I'm ready," I said very teenager'y.

"Okay, here we go," my dad said, readying his screwdriver at the first screw. Suddenly though, he shouted, "Wait!"

I jumped. "What?" I shouted in surprise.

"Maybe we should listen one more time," my dad teased as he put his face next to the AC unit and held up his hand to silence me so that he could listen.

I rolled my eyes. "Can we just fucking go already? *Please*?" I begged.

"You're so rude," my dad as he laughed at me and unscrewed the first bolt. He then crouched down and said, "I'm ready. Lift the windowpane...JUST A BIT!"

I did as instructed, and my father ever so slightly pulled the AC unit forward until it could be tilted forward into the room. As it tipped, though, we discovered we had an immediate problem on our hands. Water poured in from the unit onto him and the carpeted floor. He grimaced and through gritted teeth shouted at me, "Forget about it, just keep going!"

Following his orders, I fully raised the window. My dad let out a chuff of air as the entire weight of the AC unit rested upon him. Despite how heavy it was he continued pulling the monstrous air conditioner forward. As he did, he sort of hefted it onto his thighs and began to crab walk backwards so that I could shut the window. But as soon as he jostled the AC into the room a giant bat that had, apparently, been nesting in the air conditioner flew up and out directly toward my face.

I screamed bloody murder and let go of the window. It slammed shut and my father — who had been only momentarily prepared to bear the weight of the AC — staggered backwards into the room and was now hunched over and holding the weight of the entire thing.

He screamed my name, "Kristin! Grab it!"

I, however, ignored his shouts for help and shoved past him like a Heisman Trophy winner. I ran from the room, and I pulled the door shut behind me, which left my father alone in my bedroom with the bat.

"Kristin!" he screamed. "Get back in here!"

"I can't help you now! You're on your own," I shouted at the shut door.

I then heard in a sequence of events, a high-pitched scream; the slamming of metal into the pine paneling of my bedroom's wooden walls; loud, thudding footsteps as someone drunkenly staggered around the room; more shrieks; and then a giant crash as my father threw down the air conditioner and bolted for the door.

He spilled out of the room like Kramer in *Seinfeld* before sliding down the wall where he landed in a heap on the floor next to me. I lunged for the door and slammed it behind him.

He was out of breath like he had just been chased through a corn field for a mile.

"What are you doing?" he heaved. "How could you have just left me in there? That thing's 300 pounds."

I knelt down in front of him. He sat there stricken like Tippi Hedren in Alfred Hitchcock's *The Birds* after she's been pecked apart by crows. He flinched as I grabbed him by his shoulders. I then looked him dead in the eye, and said, "I *fucking* told you something was in that air conditioner."

This realization of truth dawned on him. "Was that the *thing* you heard *all* summer?"

"Yes!" I shouted.

His eyes widened. "Oh my gosh! What are we going to do?"

"We?!" I bellowed. "No. *You*," I said, pointing at him.

"Why me?" he challenged.

"Oh I don't know! Because you're the parent, *and* because you made sleep with a bat for the past three months."

My dad looked around, helpless. "We have to call Opa," he said, rising to his feet.

Opa, my grandfather, was my dad's father. He knew how to build or fix nearly everything. As an immigrant, he also had the work ethic of ten men and didn't suffer fools who couldn't get things done right. Once on a workday evening when he developed a toothache, he tried drilling his own tooth so he wouldn't have to miss work the following day. He, of course, nearly got blood poisoning from it, but the point is, my opa could solve anything.

"Yes," I agreed, "Opa. Call him. Immediately."

My opa arrived ten minutes later. We were in the upstairs hall.

"Wo is die Fledermaus?" he asked in German.

My father and I pointed in unison to my bedroom door.

My opa considered the situation.

"What do you need to catch it?" I asked. "A tennis racket?"

"What?" Opa asked. "No." He looked around. "This," he said, picking up the Phillips Head screwdriver that I had dropped on the floor as I flung myself from my bedroom.

"A screwdriver?" I asked.

"Ya," he said with a shrug.

He then opened my bedroom door and slipped inside like a spy in a James Bond movie — quiet and undetected. My father and I rushed over and pressed our respective ears up against the wood, but it was completely silent inside.

Less than thirty seconds had passed when my opa flung the door open, causing my dad and I to crash inside.

"Here," Opa said, in his German accent. I looked down just as he thrust the screwdriver my direction. I reeled back in horror when I saw that the bat was skewered on the other end.

"Aaaaah!" I shouted. When it slowly fluttered its webbed wings, I asked in horror, "Is it still alive?"

"Maybe," my opa observed turning the screwdriver and inspecting his handiwork, "Or maybe nerve endings." He shrugged "I will go kill him in the driveway...unless you want to, Armin."

"I think I'm good, Pop," my dad said stepping back to give my grandfather wide clearance.

In disbelief, we watched him disappear down the steps, "What is he the fucking Mr. Miyagi of bats?" I asked.

"I know!" my dad cried out in astonishment.

I say all this because I started this book by telling you that I wanted to share mostly funny stories from my life to fix us.

I'm ending it by admitting that I'm not fully sure I know how to do that. But I do know this, if we want to get closer to our abundance then we need to get *closure* to our pain. I'm not necessarily sure we need to skewer it through the heart with a screwdriver and then bludgeon it to death in the driveway....unless...well...maybe we do...but I *do* know, for sure, that we need to at the very least dissect it.

I know fixing us has become an entire industry these days. It's more heavily marketed, packaged, and promoted than a Kardashian product launch.

But that's not the form of *fixing* I'm talking about.

I mean fixing in the true way we heal actual hurt. I mean it in the way we healed after falling down as kids. We'd limp inside and a grown up, perhaps a parent, would wipe away our tears, clean our wound, maybe spray it with Bactine, put a bandage on it, and then tell us not to touch it.

"You need to let it breathe so it can heal. It'll get better. Give it time," my mom had always said.

Trauma is a bit like that. We don't need it to go away or cut it out from our history entirely. Just like we didn't cut off our whole leg when a roller-skating accident in the 2nd grade took us out.

We just need to know that it's there, be tender with it, and give it time.

I've taken up a certain belief that life is not found on the hamster wheel of becoming the best version, the new version, or the perfect version of who we are.

It is simply about becoming whole. *Whole* requires all the parts of us. Complete, broken, and in progress.

If we went to the lake and stood on the dock, and I shouted, "We have to get out of here, NOW. Pick a boat!" My guess is you'd pick the boat with both oars or all its sails, over a yacht that's missing its motor.

Trading parts of who we are because we think there is a better way to *be* is like picking the broken boat.

We are whole. The reason fix-it culture capitalizes on us is because we believe the *whole* of who we are isn't enough.

Trust me, I know, I've certainly gone done with that ship plenty of times.

But now I'm on a different cruise, one that believes that all the parts of me — the areas I like and the areas I want to evolve — are equally worthy of my love and self-acceptance.

I don't know you, but I know that things have hurt you along the way in your life because no one gets through unscathed.

I guess, all I want to say is, if one day our paths cross — and I hope they do —that you and I can find a way to laugh a little about what's made you hysterical in your life, too.

HOUSEKEEPING

Just in case, here's a bit of housekeeping:

1. My dad's feet weren't broken.
2. My mom was still wrong.
3. She will call me after reading this to rebut that statement.
4. My oma had many friends and people who loved her very much, all of whom may be surprised by what I wrote in this book. It's okay; to those of you who knew her differently than I did, you can love the version of her that you knew.
5. Speaking of my oma, I am the human I am *today* because of the ways she tested and tried me. I don't absolve her of her behavior, but I do want the Universe to know that I am aware of how all that hurt forged my humor.
6. I don't have the trunk. I wish I still had the corsage pin.
7. My father still has both his nipples; and yes, that is a line I never thought I would type...like, *ever*. In fact, I am already riddled with regret over it.
8. I realize a bat was harmed in the telling of this story. Although this was not done by my hand, I do want to make it clear that I do not condone the injury of any animal, bats included. Having said that, this is not an invitation to bats. Do not come to come my house. I still have screwdrivers.
9. I do have a new vibrator. I will not be taking it to Best Buy.

XOXO, MOXIE

This is my second book but, in some ways, it feels like a first because it is not a novel with a plotline; it is all me. In a world of criticisms, I hope this book leads to something more profound, that being connection. Thank you for picking it up and giving me a chance to do just that. Anita Ream, I knew you first as Mrs. Ream, my high school English teacher. If you had told me *then* how many times I would say the word vibrator to you, I would have been appalled. I am immensely grateful for your friendship and your editorial skills. To Natalie and the team at Pivot Creative, thank you for taking my vision and perfecting it for the book cover and layout. I am astounded by your skill. I promise next time to let you run wild. You're so very capable of it. Thank you, Mindy for your insights and input. I am grateful to have had your legal guidance and your friendship. To those whom I mention in the book or had a hand in the history of my life, I hope you know how thankful I am to each of you. To my advance readers, thank you for the support and the belief — now go write those reviews. To my extended family, I love you all and I am so lucky to have you. To my brother Brian, my sister-in-law Renee, and my niece and nephew, Noah and Maggie, you are loved beyond measure. To my ride or dies — James, Heather, Katrina, and Holly. You complete me. I am astounded by the level of belief, friendship, and laughter you bring into my life. To Jules, Sidd, and Hawk. I miss you immensely and I am so thankful I get to call you family. Erin, you are the sunshine of my life. Brooke, Gabriel, and Camp Anderson, you are my hype team. I am eternally grateful for you. Anthony, I love you from the bottom of my Eileen Fisher heart. Here's to the Two Girls and a Taco Truck Tour. Kelli, I am so thankful you found the one thing in LA you could like — me, your kinda neighbor. Veronica, Kris, Tommy, and Josh — here's to all our dreams on the horizon. Thank you for letting me swing for the fences on your behalf. Melanie, you are a dream and a half. Here's to all that is ahead. Johnnie, your guidance, belief, and support is a beacon. I am grateful to have you in my circle and corner. PJ and Chris, you are my valley girls and I love you. Thank you for always celebrating me. Bob, thank you for coming out of nowhere with a solution. You are a lifesaver. Paige, I am so thankful to have your friendship and so proud of all the talent you pour into the world. Jenni, here's to all the big dreams ahead. Only love for you. Lindsay, your friendship is a treasure. Thank you. My circle is tight, but to you Heather, Libbie, Maggie, Mary, Lesley, Becca, Kerianne, Ginger, and Lizzie, you are each a gift in my life. I am beyond lucky to call you my nearest and dearest. Thank you. To my mom and dad, I love you beyond and then some. This book is a tribute to you both. I am so very lucky to have you. All my heart, Kristin

Made in the USA
Middletown, DE
21 February 2022